Effective
Parenting

Also by the Author
WHEN YOU ARE A SINGLE PARENT

Effective Parenting:
WHAT'S YOUR STYLE?

Robert C. DiGiulio

Follett Publishing Company/Chicago

Design by Karen Yops

Library of Congress Cataloging in Publication Data

DiGiulio, Robert C   1949-
  Effective parenting.

  Bibliography: p.
  1. Parenting.   I. Title.
HQ755.83.D54   649'.1   79-26832
ISBN 0-695-81350-1

Second Printing

To my godparents,
Flora Gigante and Aldo Califano,
two very special people.
To Teresa A. Trimarco and Paul A. Robbins,
two very talented teachers.

Contents

Preface

How would you like to live with one or two strangers for at least eighteen years? What if you had absolutely no say in deciding who those people would be? And, to top it off, what if you were expected to do exactly what those one or two people wanted you to do every moment you lived with them? Would you be happy?

You'd have only two choices: You could try to escape, knowing that the police would look for you, and that when they caught you, they would bring you back to live with those people; or, you could endure living with them, follow their rules, and be like them to make them happy, in order to be permitted to do at least a few things with those eighteen years of your life. I call such a person—who must live that eighteen-year ordeal—a child.

In old Grade B movies, we've heard the petty crook say, "Some day I'm gonna bust outta dis joint!" He's living for the only thing he's got—his future. Children—especially those stuck with "bad" parents—are in the same predicament: they're future people. Although we like to think that we're preparing them for a future (career, marriage, parenthood), it's quite possible that we're preparing them to want to—first—"bust outta dis joint." Career, marriage, school, and material goods all take second place; busting out—escaping—becomes the number one priority. Make no mistake about it—it happens in "good" families, and it happens in "bad" families. And it happens because kids don't have the chance or the right to choose who their parents will be, how old they'll be, what race, religion, or income they'll have— nothing. Kids are stuck with us. They can misbehave, scream, yell, fight, plead, beg, or cry, but in the end they are powerless. Or, they can be quiet, "nice" children, obey all or most of our pronouncements, and make us proud of them by living those eighteen years doing what we think they should do. Although it sounds bleak, they have one hope.

Us. We didn't have a chance to choose our parents. But we can choose to be the kind of parents our children would choose if they were able to do so. Never mind the power we have to tell, to scold, to rule, to forbid. The only really important power that we have, that our children don't have, is the power to choose. The kind of parents we choose to be is their only hope.

Introduction

Do It in Style

Columnist Ann Landers conducted a survey recently that asked parents this question: "If you had to do it all over again, would you have children?" Of ten thousand responses, 70 percent said no.

Boston Magazine has awarded its Turkey of the Year Award to a young man who—quite seriously—named his parents in a $350,000 lawsuit for "malpractice in parenting."

A sixteen-year-old girl in California filed for divorce from her parents, citing "incompatibility." The legal ramifications of the case, which is pending, are frightening.

According to the latest National Education Association teacher opinion poll, discipline is the most pressing problem facing the schools. Furthermore, according to the poll, irresponsible parents and unsatisfactory home conditions are the main causes for the behavior problems in the schools.

The public agrees with the teachers' assessments. According to the most recent *Gallup Poll of the Public's Attitudes Toward the Public Schools,* discipline heads the list of problems facing our schools. In fact, the percentage of poll respondents naming discipline was the highest since these annual surveys began ten years ago.

George Gallup, originator of the prestigious poll, pointed to the need for parental assertiveness: "It is probably no exaggeration to say that the next great advance in education will come when parents and teachers work as a team, with parents taking full responsibility for problems that arise in the home."

But the role of the parent cannot and should not be simply to head off problems in the home. We know that the best way to cope with problems is to prevent them from happening. Fine. But where can we start to "work as a team," as suggested by Mr. Gallup? What help can we parents get by looking to the schools?

First of all, any successful elementary school teacher or high school teacher who has had a few years' experience in the classroom would agree with the following two statements:

What the adult in charge does—or doesn't do—is crucial to the kinds of behaviors seen in the classroom.

A teacher who is a screamer in the classroom is very definitely setting a certain tone; likewise, a parent who is constantly yelling at home can expect the child to tune out or to respond with either meek or aggressive behavior. On the other hand, a parent or teacher who comes across as a pushover or a softie will cause a different reaction than a Hitler or a real grind.

The best discipline is preventive discipline.

As I said before, the best way to cope with problems is to prevent them from happening. This is sometimes difficult to achieve, but it is absolutely the surest way to a class that runs smoothly, where children can learn uninterrupted by their own misbehavior and the antics of their classmates. Teachers who take the time and make the effort to set up their classrooms in a way that leads to preventive discipline often find that their success with this technique hinges on their own behavior when teaching in class. Successful teachers have evaluated themselves carefully and have worked at making changes—sometimes drastic changes—in their style. These changes might involve mannerisms, pet phrases, glances, attitudes, or even clothing. The significant factor is that the teachers made changes in themselves before they attempted to make changes in their students. And there's no doubt that examining style is vital for parents, too.

Let's look at the schools for one more example. Effective teachers have learned that talking doesn't always work; silence is often a more effective way to deal with certain kinds of misbehavior. Teachers who have tuned in to style have no magic wands; they have no special inborn gifts or genius abilities, but they do have an effective, well-developed style that can carry them through a potentially explosive situation, a style that they know is working, and, in the case of some high school teachers, a style that helps them deal with up to two hundred different children each day, every day, in a healthy, positive way. They have learned to scrap a technique that doesn't work and try another. In short, they have learned how to see their ineffective style, and they have made important changes in their own behaviors that almost guarantee that their problems will decrease—not necessarily disappear—freeing them to get on with teaching. Think of all the teachers you had in school. There are probably only a few—too few, sadly—who stand out as teachers who had style. You could use every possible adjective to describe them: warm, caring, good but not harsh disciplinarian, fair, human—the list could go on and on. They weren't born that way!

Just as these teachers had a positive impact on the children in their classes, you can be the kind of parent who has a healthy impact on the children in your life. Parents can develop their styles in the same fashion as effective teachers. I hope to spare you some of the agony of trial and error.

"Why Do We Keep Doing That?"

We parents are often too quick to consult psychologists or psychiatrists when confronted with a behavior problem. Unnecessary consultations are useful only in yielding terms like *neurosis, acting out, frustrated, hyperactive,* or any of a thousand possibilities. Certainly, there are times when professional services are necessary, but if we seek professional help in shouldering a responsibility that is ours and ours alone, we're giving up that responsibility to someone who is not always in the best position to make important changes in our children. Who is? As parents, we are.

We've all heard some of the horror stories connected with watching television.

More time is spent watching television by a preschooler than the equivalent of six years of schooling.

By the time a child is eighteen, he or she will have spent the equivalent of two full years of life in front of the tube—more time than in any other activity except sleeping.

By the time the child is twenty-one, he or she will have seen more than 250,000 commercials.

In addition to worrying about the amount of time our children spend captivated by the television, we can justly think about the influence of TV. Whether it's a "good" influence or a "bad" influence, it's certainly not our influence. We, as parents, have absolutely no control over what's on television, and whether we like it or not, our children watch television and are influenced by it. We're turning our responsibility over to Mister Rogers or Ronald McDonald. They can't instill good behavior habits in our children—but we can.

We rely on teachers, too. Sometimes we rely on them when we should not. ("Don't those teachers teach you how to behave?" we say angrily.) Parents must work with the teacher; parents should take an active interest in school; teachers should support the behaviors taught at home. Fine. We've all heard these sayings many times. But, should teachers—indeed, can they—take the responsibility that is ours as parents?

"Why do we keep doing that?" Doing what? Not making changes in our behavior that will help us function as more effective parents. We know our children better than any teacher, doctor, or television scriptwriter will ever know them; and we are in the best position to take advantage of that opportunity.

Do You Have to Be Dead First in Order to Be a Good Undertaker?

When I was in graduate school, some of the students in my counseling program believed very strongly that in order to be an effective counselor and make some real changes in a client's self-defeating behavior, one must first have undergone therapy or, at the very least, seen a psychologist for treatment of a pressing personal problem. I was always tempted to ask, "Do lawyers need to be arrested and put on trial before they can be effective lawyers?" or, "Do you have to be dead first in order to be a good undertaker?"

Despite what we hear and read, and despite current fashionable thinking, a concerned mother does not have to take up jogging around the block herself before she tries to help her overweight daughter. A father need not get rid of all his angry impulses (as if that were possible) before he takes action toward helping his son stop fighting with other children. We need not become totally competent in everything we do in order to raise healthy, well-adjusted children. If that were the case, we should throw in the towel right now. If we wait for perfection within ourselves as parents before making positive changes in our children's behavior, we will wait forever and should give up even the idea of having children. Perfection, or being an ideal role model, is not necessary or possible, but being in control of those simple styles that we can look at and change is necessary—and possible!

There is no one definitive rule that will, if followed faithfully, insure success in parenting. But, whether you're married with four children or a single parent with two, one thing is certain: To control your children's behavior, you must be able to control your own behavior toward your children. Problems aren't problems until they're out of control. A good driver keeps the car under control; accidents occur when cars go out of control. A competent teacher's class is never out of control. The actor, surgeon, or hair stylist is in control of what he or she is doing. That's the kind of control I'm talking about. Just as the accomplished teacher has developed a style that enables him or her to be in control, the model parent is one who has made some important changes in order to develop an effective style when dealing with children.

If you are to derive any benefit from these pages, you must be willing to take a close look at your style and see how your behavior patterns (styles) may stand in the way of your best efforts toward raising well-behaved children. If you do not feel that you can change some of your behaviors, if you do not have the confidence to try different strategies at home, if you are afraid of children, if you think that love alone will solve behavior problems, if you take misbehavior as a personal insult, if you think that your children are just impossible, or if you think that school will teach them good behavior, then you'll probably be better off without children; merely surviving parenthood may be a challenge for you.

Being a parent is a terribly difficult career. Some parents find the times they spend with their children to be an eternity; getting through the day can be a real chore. Other parents sometimes feel let down; they want to be even better for their children but are not sure how to go about it. If, at times, you feel impotent as a parent—powerless, incapable, inefficient, or just about disabled—think how a child feels when he or she needs to look to you for limits, for structure. Does the child feel lost? By examining the styles discussed in part 1, you can learn to help yourself and, most of all, your children.

What Is Good Behavior?

Before I discuss the different parent-styles and the effects those styles have on children's behavior, it's important to try to define what I mean by "good behavior." Like love or happiness, good behavior is difficult to define. What one parent considers good behavior might be unacceptable behavior to another, and a third parent might be in disagreement with the first two.

With these variations in mind, I've come up with a definition of good behavior that I've drawn from my experience as a teacher, principal, counselor, and parent. And I think it's broad enough to allow it to be acceptable to most parents: Good behavior permits children to live in harmony with their parents, friends, other adults, and, most of all, with themselves. The key word in this definition is *harmony*.

Unfortunately (or fortunately), there are no set procedures a child or adult can follow that will guarantee good behavior. It's not like tuning an engine or making a devil's food cake, in that no simple, step-by-step instructions or recipes are available. And that's what makes being a parent such a challenging, sometimes difficult occupation. We know what we want (good behavior), but we can't pull out a manual or a file card with specific instructions on how to get it. But, in a way, that's the best part!

Why? For one reason, children will grow up in a world full of different people—people who will have different expectations, people who will act in different ways toward your child. A child brought up according to a fixed, rigid set of rules will most likely be unable to deal flexibly with adults of different values and different persuasions.

For another good reason, a cookbook approach to seeking good behavior will stunt the child's ability to live harmoniously with himself or herself. People have feelings, whether they're adults or children, and behavior is a manifestation of those feelings. We want our children to be free to use the rules and guidelines we've set up, not so much for our happiness but so that our children can express their feelings and their personalities in ways acceptable and productive to themselves and their world.

Extending the original definition a bit further, then: Good behavior will allow a child to grow into an adult who lives harmoniously with other adults and children.

We parents are working toward good behavior in our children not only for the now (so we can be proud of our children) but also for the future, when they will need to be effective adults, able to control and direct their energies toward goals that will help them to meet their needs, to lead happy, full lives. We want to prepare them to be acceptable to their contemporaries and to be productive—for themselves and for their society. These two words, then, *acceptable* and *productive*, are the cornerstones of that mysterious structure called good behavior.

Productive behavior allows a child to build, to construct, to achieve, to capitalize on strengths, and, generally, to utilize his or her energy positively. In school, we try to teach good study habits in order that children make the best use of information presented, that they learn—regardless of whether this learning is directed toward producing an original limerick, a critical book review, or a colorful mobile. At home, productive behavior can include anything from using crayon and paper to fine-tuning the engine on a dirt bike. Although there is no specific list of productive behaviors, the different kinds could number in the millions.

Unproductive behavior is a destructive, wasteful, and negative utilization of a child's energy. It isn't satisfying to the child, nor does it contribute anything to the family, parents, school, or society. Just as I could list a million productive behaviors, I could list a million and one unproductive behaviors. Any parent can.

Just as we want to guide children toward productive utilization of their energy, we want our children, or, more specifically, our children's behavior, to be acceptable—acceptable to the child and acceptable to the adult world. Manners are a simple example of acceptable behavior—when they're good manners, of course. We teach our children to use a fork instead of fists with spaghetti because forks are acceptable, fists aren't. That's an obvious example. When we get away from the obvious acceptable behaviors, the whole idea of what's acceptable becomes a tricky subject because each of us has a somewhat different idea of what is, and isn't, acceptable behavior.

Following are examples of how parents pass along this-is-acceptable-behavior messages to their children.

The mother of one of my daughter's playmates came into my living room and told little Debra, "It's time to come home." When she took her daughter's hand, the five-year-old kicked her mother in the legs, screaming, "No, no, no . . . I want to stay! I want to stay!" Not only was this behavior unproductive, but it was also—to most reasonable parents—unacceptable. Unfortunately, Debra's mother made it acceptable, when, after being kicked—hard—in the shins, she turned to me and said, "Well, she's got to express her feelings." Incredible? Not at all.

Sometimes parents go to the other extreme. A mother picked up her son from my school at ten o'clock to take him to the dentist. He not only wanted to stay in school, but, even more, he wanted no part of the unpleasantness he associated with going to the dentist. As I walked them out toward the front door, the boy started to cry. He didn't kick, scream, or resist; he just cried—copiously. Mother stopped and warned him, in no uncertain terms, to "cut it out" right away. She made his behavior of crying an unacceptable act, though it was a legitimate expression of his feelings. That's the other side to the word *acceptable*.

We need to permit children to express their feelings in acceptable ways, without letting that expression turn into the unacceptable actions like kicking, fighting, or destroying. It's a thin line for us parents to walk as we keep in mind the fact that we are directly influencing our children's behavior. We're the ones who are letting children know by our words, actions, or silence that what they are doing is either good behavior or bad behavior—acceptable and productive or unacceptable and unproductive.

The fact that children's behavior is so closely tied to, and influenced by, our parental behavior has led me to one of the major points of this book. I call this point the first precept.

The First Precept

Nothing in this book is carved in stone—except the first precept: The majority of disciplinary problems your child might have is caused or worsened, directly or indirectly, by your behavior. Your ineffective and inappropriate styles are, in most cases, launching pads for your child's problem behavior. You are responsible for bringing your child into a wholesome, stimulating, controlled environment. You are the behavior engineer whose job is, on one level, to raise children with appropriate behavior habits and, ultimately, to help your children gain control of their lives, their selves. It is crucial, then, that you be aware of your style. How well you can work with your style is the key ingredient to how your child behaves, views you, views other adults, and, ultimately, views himself or herself as an adult. Since a child is powerless, all he or she can do is respond to your style, not help you change it or force you to do so. It's in your hands—you can break the vicious circle!

You can accept the fact that your style of behavior deeply affects your child's behavior. And, if you're like most parents, you want to teach your child to have good behavior. You want well-behaved children. Briefly, let's take a look at how we convey those messages of good or bad behavior—how parents teach.

Negative Teaching: The Devious Don'ts

If we examine the ways we deal with our children, it might interest, amaze, or shock us to realize that most of the time we're not teaching them how to behave; we're teaching them how not to behave! To illustrate this negative teaching, let me give you examples of what I call the devious don'ts:

> Don't do that.
> Don't chew with your mouth open.
> Don't you hear me?
> Don't be home too late!
> Don't bother me.

Don't answer back.
Don't pull the cat's tail.

With the devious don'ts, we really don't teach anything. After a few years, children know what they're not supposed to do, but they often don't know what they are supposed to do. Put yourself, for a moment, in a child's place. You've just gotten a job in a bewilderingly large factory. You don't know what is made there or what your job is, but you know you're supposed to do something. You gingerly pull a handle on the machine before you, and the supervisor runs over and says, "Don't do that!" When you let go, the handle falls off. "Now look at what you've done! You shouldn't have touched it!" you're told. "But what am I supposed to do?" you ask. "Do as you're told!" You persist: "But you haven't told me anything!" "Don't answer back!"

So you go back to your business, whatever it might be, still ignorant of what's expected of you. At least now you know you're not supposed to touch the machine. You grab a broom, because the floor is dirty, and you sweep. The supervisor descends on you, telling you, "Stop! Don't do that—it's not your job!" Grabbing the broom from you, the supervisor leaves. You've learned just two things: don't touch the machine, and don't touch the broom.

Positive Teaching: The Delightful Dos

I'm certainly not saying that you should eliminate the word *don't* from your parental vocabulary, but use it in moderation, and always tie a positive *do* to it. Here's how.

Your child pulls the cat's tail. You might say, "Don't pull the cat's tail." Fine. But that's just half the job of teaching good behavior. Take a moment more to pick up the kitty and show your child how to stroke a cat gently on the head and scratch under the cat's chin. This is the "do" half of teaching good, acceptable, and productive behavior. And we parents teach positive dos by our actions as well as by our words.

Recently, I saw an excellent example of positive teaching without words at a local Pizza Hut restaurant. A boy—eight or nine years old—was about to bite into a juicy piece of pizza that had just been delivered to his table. Just as he brought the slice of pizza to his lips, he lost his grip on it, and the whole piece fell into his lap. Disgusted, he rested his head in both hands, elbows planted on the table. Instead of saying, "Don't get mad," or "Don't you know how to eat pizza?" his father grabbed a napkin and helped clean the boy's lap. Without saying a word, his mother put another piece on his plate and cut it into a few little pieces. As she placed a knife and fork on the plate, the boy looked up at her, smiled, and said, "Why didn't I think of that?"

Sure, it takes patience. But emphasizing the positive, the dos, pays off. The behavior of the parents is the key to good behavior on the part of the child. Had the Pizza Hut parents behaved differently, the child would have reacted differently. You don't have to be perfect. Being positive is all any child could ask of you.

In fact, if I had to name the single most important thing a parent could do for his or her child, I'd say, "Give your child a chance to be good." I'm not saying you should give your children material things, nor do I advocate giving them the world on a silver platter. Just give them, through your words and actions, the chance to feel good about themselves—the chance to take pride in their growing ability to direct their lives toward goals that are worthwhile and the chance to be productive and accepted human beings now and as adults. A chance to be good. That's what this book is all about.

Part One—**PARENT-STYLES**

1
Six Parent-Styles— and Style Seven

The most potent socializing force so far discovered appears to be children learning through observing what others do— particularly parents.

—Dr. Charles Schaefer

To say that there are precisely six styles of parenting would be misleading, since no parent is strictly a single-style person. Each parent has a predominant style and one or more strong styles, which are helpful indicators of some of the ways he or she relates to the child. In a similar vein, it would be wrong to say that there are only six styles of parenting, because each parent has a unique manner, a unique way of carrying out his or her style when dealing with children. We're stressing what's similar rather than what's different. Parent-styles are not labels; just because you know your parent-style does not mean that you—as an individual—are fully described by that style.

For example, the famous French painter Cezanne and the Dutch painter Van Gogh were both Postimpressionistic in their styles, but their individual works were certainly unique. They belong to the same school of painting because most art experts feel the aesthetic effects of much of their painting are similar. Just like art—the effects of a parent-style are, indeed, similar!

What causes a particular style—where does it come from? Parent-styles are ways we behave toward our children, which, to a large extent, are ways we've learned. Our most effective teachers have been our parents—for better or for worse. Not one person is a born parent; we learn how to be parents. Although some researchers believe that women are born with an innate ability to mother, and men with an ability to father, not one person is born with the ability to be a parent—much less to be a creative, wonderful, loving, caring, and sensitive one. We learn how to be parents largely through our own experiences as children. Have you ever reacted to annoying behavior from your husband by saying something like, "Just like your mother—same bad habits"? Or, when your wife gives in to the children, do you say, "You're a pushover—just like your mother"?

If you take a careful look at yourself, you can certainly see many aspects of your behavior, positive and negative, that are direct hand-me-downs from Mom and Pop. The secret in recognizing your parent-style is this: Hold on to the wonderful behaviors you've gotten from your parents—the kindness, the generosity, the many little things that you know are special about you as a parent. The very last thing you'd want to do would be to eliminate those strong, positive traits. Write them down; set them aside. Now prepare yourself to take a good close look at some styles, and think of the ways you feel unsuccessful as a mother or father—the ways in which you know you need to change.

Historical Background: Before There Were Styles

Interest in what I call parent-styles can be traced to 1928, when the behavioral scientists J. B. Watson and R. R. Watson warned parents against showing too much love toward their children. Many parents took this to heart; the Depression that followed probably made such a cut-and-dried approach to parenting both possible and advisable. Those were lean years, indeed, for parents and children.

Interest in parent-styles was rekindled in 1941 by psychologist H. Champney, and in the post–World War II years, by researchers such as Baldwin, Kalhorn, and Breese. Their work indicated that parents seem to show syndromes or clusters of behavior toward children, and the words *democratic* and *indulgent* were used. About six years later, Crandall and Preston identified parents who consistently use coercive control when dealing with children. In 1945 child psychologist G. G. Lafore classified parents into four groups: dictators, cooperators, temporizers, and appeasers.

As might be expected, these labels never caught on, and just two terms became very popular words to describe parental behavior: *strict* and *permissive* were the buzz words of the 1950s.

After those words came into general use, researchers began to look into the ways strict and permissive parents influenced the behavior of their children. Although no answers were clear cut, it seemed that children from permissive parents were friendlier to other children, showed more creative ideas, more easily expressed their feelings, and showed less conformity than children from strict homes. Children from restricted (strict) homes were more inhibited in their behavior; they seemed to be less playful but more obedient than children from permissive homes. Children from democratic (another term that appeared in the 1950s) homes and democratic parents tended to be active and more effective in their relationships with other children. These studies showed that the behavior pattern (or style) of the parent has a decided effect upon the child, but that that effect, naturally, depends on the style of the parent. Words such as *democratic, permissive,* and *strict* have become so overused that they don't mean very much anymore. Besides, we all know parents who are permissive at times and quite strict at other times—depending on the circumstances.

More recently, the Parental Authority Research Project (University of California at Berkeley) looked at some of the characteristics of preschool children and at three types, or styles, of parenting: authoritative, authoritarian, and permissive. The preferred style was the first; authoritative parents seemed to be healthy, adult leaders. The permissive parents were permissive in the traditional sense—the parent is hesitant to use his or her authority, and the child is the center of the disciplinary structure. At the other end, the authoritarian parent had a dominating, dictatorial style of parenting. As might be expected, the authoritarian style was not seen as a desirable parent-type at all.

Seven Parent-Styles

Regardless of the particular words used to describe the parent's style of behavior, it's generally accepted that parents often respond to children (and to other adults) in fixed ways.

What I'm presenting here is a new way to look not only at the different styles parents assume when dealing with children, but also at how those styles affect the behavior of their children. My seven style categories incorporate more of the parent's observable actions and modus operandi into the whole process of child behavior. I am not saying that if, for example, a parent is a martyr-style parent, he or she will have martyr-style children. But if a parent operates as a martyr-style parent, certain stereotyped behaviors are likely to result—in parent and in child. I've referred to these behaviors as fallout—how our styles affect children.

As you read through each of the following six chapters, you will get a clearer idea as to why each style category received its name. But, for now, a brief explanation is in order.

The *child-style parent* is a parent who, in the words of Peter Pan, "won't grow up." With extreme sympathy and compassion for the viewpoint and the feelings of the child, the child-style parent relates to children as child-to-child, and not as adult- or parent-to-child.

The *doctor-style parent* must find out "Why? What's the diagnosis?" Often cold and clinical, and sometimes cynical, the doctor-style parent has an almost doctor-to-patient relationship with a child—adult-to-adult, instead of adult-to-child.

The doctor-style parent is so named for his or her clinical, diagnosis-seeking manner. Doctors are no more doctor-style parents than child-style parents are actually little children.

There is no better word to describe the parent who is an appeaser and a child-pleaser than *diplomat*. The *diplomat-style parent* seeks—at all costs—to maintain a peaceful, placid relationship with the child, even using blatant bribery if needed.

In the good old days, we called parents who ruled with an iron hand disciplinarians or authoritarians. I call them *autocrat-style parents,* some of whom could make a dictator knuckle under.

Pity the poor *martyr-style parent,* trudging through this vale of tears as a sacrificial lamb to the altar of parenthood! The martyr-style mother, for example, will cut a pie into fourths and save the fifth piece for herself. Extreme sacrifice, doing without for-the-good-of-the-child, and "God, give me strength; what did I do to deserve this?" are the creeds by which the martyr-parent lives. (Groucho Marx might have said, "You call that living?")

The *talker-style parent,* whose children have the best-developed ears in town, relies to an extraordinary extent on words rather than actions, silence, gestures, or nonverbal forms of communication. The talker-style parent talks—but communicates? Never.

The *style-seven parent* is not the ideal parent; however, this parent is effectively helping children grow as productive and accepted full human beings. The style-seven parent is not perfect but is growing conscious of the effect his or her behavior, words, and attitudes have on children—not perfect but trying to change for the better all the time.

One more important point about your parent-style: All of us parents need to remember that we are our children's first contact with the great big world out there. And, as I've said before, the ways we behave toward our children and with our children set the stage for their entry into the world. I am not saying that your child will turn out as a carbon copy of you. But I am saying that you have a profound effect on your child—an effect that can be used to help your child function and grow as a happy, healthy human being, or an effect that will serve to hinder him or her. How your child relates to the world is not up to the school, the government, grandpa, or grandma; it's up to you. Yes, your spouse will have an equally powerful effect. But you can look at and change some of your own ineffective and sometimes harmful behaviors. If you're successful, work with your spouse on your combined styles. Essentially, though, it's only you who can help yourself.

Again, remember that you are your child's first contact with society, with people. Let it be a positive, constructive, and fruitful contact.

The following chapters describe each parent-style, and they speak to the kinds of fallout (child behavior) we can expect within each style. These styles and fallout should not be seen as bad or wrong; there's really no right or wrong way to be in the business of parenting. There are parental actions or words that produce desirable results, and there are those that produce undesirable results. Use the following chapters (and especially part 2) not only to take a look at your styles but also to learn how you can make some healthy, positive changes that will produce desirable and beneficial results for you and for your children.

The late Dr. Albert Schweitzer, mission doctor, theologian, philosopher, musician, and Nobel Peace Prize winner, summed up the importance of parental behavior. When asked about the best way for parents to raise well-behaved children, he answered, "There are three ways: by example, by example, and by example."

2
The
Child-Style
Parent

Youth can grow old and not grow wise.

—Japanese Proverb

A Child-Style Adult: Sally Ryan*

Sally is a twenty-five-year-old mother of two girls. She's a teacher's aide, in charge of the children while they wait for the school bus and during recess. Sally is well liked by the children, parents, and teachers, but she is having a great deal of difficulty with her job. Controlling the children is a challenge for her because they don't listen to her. At the beginning of the school year, Sally and the children had a good talk about what was allowed and what wasn't. But now it seems that much has been forgotten.

---

*All names and circumstances used to illustrate the different parent styles and parent-style statements have, of course, been changed to prevent any parental embarrassment—and to help me keep my job!

While she was supervising one group of children, a fight broke out on the other side of the playground. When Sally ordered one of the fighters to "Go to your teacher and tell him what you did," the fighter's friends ganged up and accused Sally of being unfair for punishing one child and not the other. After numerous calls from angry parents, Sally quit her job, feeling that she received no support from the teachers or from the school administration. Sally operates as a child-style adult.

A Child-Style Parent: John Howland

John Howland is a man who can be relied upon to set up a baseball team for the neighborhood children, assist the cub scouts by driving groups of noisy boys to hiking spots, or hold a barbecue every summer for his four children and their friends. Not one person has a bad word to say about John—except his wife.

"You're letting the kids walk all over you, and you don't care. Face facts, John. You spoil them—anything they want, they get. It's not good; they have to learn sometime that they can't get whatever they want whenever they want it. Furthermore, I'm sick of being the 'bad guy.' Take your share of disciplining them for a change!"

He knows she's right. As a matter of fact, he has felt pressured by his kids lately, and worrying about his job hasn't helped. His oldest son, Johnny Jr., is nineteen and hasn't worked a day yet; he depends on his dad for all his money. John loves his children deeply; he really doesn't mind giving, and even supporting his oldest son.

John was comfortable with his wife's role as the children's disciplinarian until recently, when it became obvious that the three younger children practically wreck the house when she's not home. John is puzzled and hurt. He's a good provider; even though the kids are often disobedient, they know that Dad loves them. He doesn't know what to do. John is a child-style parent.

What's a Child-Style Parent?

Some unpleasant examples of extreme child-style parents were caricatured on television in the 1950s—Gracie Allen ("The Burns and Allen Show") and Dagwood Bumstead ("Blondie") were innocent child-parents. Harmless, helpful, usually inept, these characters were followed by poor, sweet Edith Bunker, Archie's wife in "All in the Family." Child-style parents, it would seem, are naturals for television, since they can be portrayed without strong passions, dominating emotions, or deep worries. In short, they are depicted as unreal people at whom we can freely laugh—simpletons, dingbats, and victims. The child-style parent is not in the least a simpleton or a dingbat, but he or she is a victim.

Just as children are almost totally powerless in most institutions—school, church, home, scouts—the child-style parent is usually powerless in his or her role as an adult and as a parent. Generally, child-style parents do not have a consistent way of dealing with behavior problems; their responses are governed by the particular situation. If they are confronted with a behavior problem, confusion reigns—they're not really sure what to do. They tend to act according to how they feel at that moment. More than thirty years ago, G. G. Lafore wrote "Practices of Parents in Dealing with Preschool Children," in which she described such parents as "temporizers"—parents whose approach to children depends on the situation. Similarly, child-style parents do not usually have any clear ideas or firm convictions concerning how to go about raising their children. They just want to do a good job and show lots of love.

If anything, this belief that loving the child will somehow translate into good behavior is the particular downfall of the child-style parent.

When confronted with a frustrating behavior problem, the child-style mother might threaten, "Wait until your father gets home," since there is little that the mother can do to enforce the limits that have been set. If the child is doing something forbidden, such as touching Mother's fine china, the child-style father might say, "I don't think Mommy wants you to do that," in much the same way that an older brother might lend advice. No discipline, lots of advice.

The child-style parent will usually draw attention to feelings rather than actions. "You hurt my feelings," says the child-style mother to her daughter. "Okay, you can have one more chance," the child-style father tells his son for the third time. After making up with his son, the child-style father is likely to shake hands and say, "We're still friends, right?"

Guilt is one of the most potent tools used by a child-style parent, though it's used in an impotent, childish manner. "Now see what you've made me do" or "You'll pay for this" are typical responses of a child-style parent to a misbehaving child—little action and little real power.

Finally, child-style parents feel most threatened when risking the disapproval of the child. In other words, the child-style parent desperately needs the approval of the child in almost any action taken by the parent. He or she does not want to do anything to which the child could say, "You're not being fair!" To accuse the child-style parent of being unfair is to deal a devastating blow. As such, it is one of the best ways a child can control his or her child-style parent.

Child-Style Fallout: A Sympathetic Sharing of Powerlessness

Although the child of a child-style parent feels a great deal of love, warmth, and sincerity and knows he or she can get just about anything from such a parent, the child-style parent is unconsciously engaged in a competition with the child and, thus, is in a battle for control. "My child never listens to me" is one of the most common complaints of the child-style parent.

Because the parent has given up control to the child, he or she relies on the other parent or on other adults, such as teachers, or, in severe cases, police, for enforcing rules. Sometimes the child gets away with murder, prompting other adults (who are not child-styles) to remark, "He's really such a nice, loving child. Too bad his mother can't control him."

The child-style parent's great love for the child demands that the child's approval—not acceptance—be sought before just about anything can be done. "Put on your socks, okay?" is the command of a child-style parent to a preschooler. "We're still friends, right?" says the child-style father after an upset with his child. The problem is that the command of a child-style parent sounds like a request to the child. The child's natural response is sometimes "I don't want to" or, simply, "No." Is the child being defiant? Probably not, because he or she is used to being asked and not told.

In one case, a child-style parent prohibited her son from going out to play because his sister was sick, and since she had to stay in, so did her healthy brother. Naturally, a big argument followed, since the son thought this was unfair. The child-style mother wanted to be fair; her daughter's accusation of "It's not fair for him to go outside" had a telling effect on the decision Mother made—a classical child-style parent decision.

Love causes big problems for both child and child-style parent. The famous Swiss psychologist Jean Piaget referred to love as "the American problem." The idea that love conquers all is a peculiarly American idea—one that springs from the American sympathy for the little guy, the victim, and the downtrodden. There's no doubt in the mind of the child-style parent that love is absolutely the most important element in raising children. Let's look at some child-and-parent behavior that helps illustrate this notion.

Recently, Robert had a birthday party at school. Sara, his mother, brought in seven exquisite cakes, beautifully and painstakingly decorated. I said, "These cakes are incredible! Where do you find the time to bake them?" Sara confessed that she had stayed up for the past three nights to work on the cakes after the children went to bed. She got only two hours' sleep each night before she had to get ready for work the next morning. Sara felt compelled to bake the cakes because she had provided similar parties for Robert's three brothers, and she loved Robert "just as much." What Sara didn't realize was that she had gradually become caught in a love trap. With each birthday, each occasion, she felt compelled to give each of the four children exactly what the others got. She felt that her love was at stake and that she had to keep proving her love to her children.

Sara's children were pulling the strings. She had absolutely no control over them. Sara was behaving in a classical child-style manner. She placed herself in a position of a big kid who was vulnerable in the sense that she could be called not fair, and thus operated on the same level as her four children.

The following September, two of Sara's four boys were placed in a remedial reading setting, receiving extra help from our reading aide for one period per day. They enjoyed working with the aide, and the other two boys (who did not need that extra help) resented this. Sara called me and asked why two of her boys were "not allowed" to be with Mrs. Finch. I explained that the two boys who were getting the extra help needed it, and the other two didn't. She understood but asked me what she should do when the boys who weren't getting extra help complained to her that it wasn't fair that they couldn't go to Mrs. Finch, too.

I asked Sara to come in, and with the four boys present, I went over the reasons why some children need extra help. This seemed to solve the problem in school, but not at home. After meeting with Sara and talking to her on the telephone, I realized the frightful proportions of the domination of this child-style mother. She was trying to cope with tremendous expectations placed on her by an uncaring husband, a full-time job, read-me-a-story requests each night from each of the children, and bitter quarrels. This woman was being racked in her effort to prove that she loved her children. I advised Sara to seek professional help and recommended a local family agency.

Fortunately, few children and child-style parents get into situations as bad as Sara's. Parents can often draw the line—by blowing their lids and saying, "Enough! Here's where I draw the line," by seeking help through therapy or individual counseling, or by making a concerted effort to control some of those out-pourings of love. The child-style parent who gets caught in the love trap usually has little problem when the child is a toddler, but trouble begins when the child turns six or seven. And the problem doesn't let up throughout adolescence and adulthood. Bad behavior on the part of the child is seen as the parent's, not the child's, fault—"You made me act bad because you don't love me." The noted psychologist Bruno Bettelheim summed it all up in the title of one of his excellent books, *Love Is Not Enough*. For the child-style parent, love (or what seems like love) is a downright dangerous weapon. And children are the ones who wield that weapon—with amazing cunning and accuracy.

The children of child-style parents often realize that they can get one more chance when they've misbehaved. For example, if a child has not cleaned up his or her room—knowing that it's a prerequisite for going out to play—he or she might plead for one more chance. If the punishment for fighting is to get sent to the bedroom, the fighters can often plead for another chance "not to fight" if the parent does not invoke the punishment. Children can pick up on this, knowing that the ax won't fall and that chances will keep coming. One more chance is given for the second, third, fourth time because "This hurts me more than it hurts you."

Just as a child is powerless and can only live either for immediate gratification or for the far future, so, too, is the child-style parent. There's a sympathetic sharing of powerlessness. Neither child nor parent feels in full control of power, and a continuous struggle develops to gain what power can be gotten—power over the other person, and little else.

3

The
Doctor-Style
Parent

Ask me no questions, and I'll tell you no fibs.

—Oliver Goldsmith

Doctor-Style Parents: Paul and Audrey Collins

Chris Collins is a seventh-grade student who graduated from my school's sixth grade last year. A bright boy, Chris presented no discipline problem to our staff, though he was one of our underachievers. This year, his first in junior high school, Chris has been in trouble ever since the first day of school—disrespect, disobedience, and now vandalism. His parents—professional people—are well read, articulate, and seemingly A1 parents. They made almost every parent-teacher conference and supported the teacher, the PTA, and the school. Their interest in Chris's welfare and success in life was evident.

39

The junior high school principal called me to ask about my experiences with Chris, and all I could say was that I had had no problems with him at all. He asked if I'd talk to Chris, since he was getting nowhere, and both he and Chris's parents were "very perplexed."

When Chris stopped by my office after school, he sat down and told me what had been happening. "I quit the gymnastics team, my grades are almost all failures now, and my friends are different—I hang out with a different group now." I asked about his parents, what their reaction to this change had been. Chris began to cry. He said, "I'm sick of my goddamned perfect parents. Nothing they do is ever wrong—just what I do is wrong.

"Mr. Di, you don't really know them like I do. They're always polite to you to show you how sophisticated they are. They always want to talk. I'm sick of talking things out, especially with my father."

Chris felt that his family "isn't real" because his parents "never argue, never have any fights," and he was positive that they really didn't love each other, or him. His home was—as he saw it—too perfect.

Chris had suffered at the hands of a father (and possibly mother, too) with a very strong doctor-style. He felt that his home was almost clinical, with much discussion, attempts at sincerity, but little gut-level love. No screaming or arguing, but little jumping for joy, either.

A Doctor-Style Parent: Neil Phillips

Neil Phillips is one of the most valued architects in his firm, Cantfall Associates. His successful, organized presentations have brought a tremendous amount of business to his company, and he has found answers to architectural problems thought impossible to solve.

Neil got married when he was thirty because he thought it was time to start thinking about raising a family. His son is now four, and his daughter is six. Neil sometimes wonders why he wanted to have a family at all.

One of the worst "crimes" his wife can commit is to ask Neil to stay with the children when she spends Saturday out with her friends. He feels guilty because he is bored with his children's company; his mind wanders to that dramatic presentation he made last Tuesday or to this Monday's business trip. He also feels his children are a burden to his zooming career. In college, Neil took up psychology and tries now to get his children to express their feelings and not to keep them bottled up inside. He feels torn because he wants to be the kind of perfect parent he never had. Neil has difficulty understanding why his children seem like such a burden. After a long discussion with his wife, Neil has decided to see a private counselor to help him sort out his mixed feelings toward being a parent. Neil is a doctor-style parent.

What's a Doctor-Style Parent?

If anyone is to be held accountable for our unfortunate tendency to treat children like adults, it's the doctor-style parent. A child's illogical ways of arriving at a conclusion are totally mystifying to this type of parent, who feels that children should be logical, rational creatures. The doctor-style parent seeks an answer for the child's problems and, if it's a behavior problem, sometimes has difficulty seeing how he or she—as a parent—is part of the problem and the solution.

The doctor-style parent's favorite word is *why*. When confronted with misbehavior, he or she often embarks on a one-to-one crusade to find the answer to why.

PARENT: Why did you hit your sister?

CHILD: (No response—doesn't really know why.)

PARENT: Did you hear me? Why did you do that?

CHILD: Because she called me a name.

PARENT: Why did she call you a name?

CHILD: Because . . . I . . . I don't know.

PARENT: Why don't you know? (And so on.)

The doctor-style parent wants to talk to his or her children, wants to keep the lines of communication open. Thus, the doctor-style parent is usually more successful with older children than with toddlers. Since the doctor-style parent tries to be "with it," he or she realizes the importance of communicating feelings and of using buzz words like *relating* and *rapping*.

However, the doctor-style parent is traditional in most other respects; in many ways he or she seeks to be the kind, sensitive parent he or she never had—a very traditional wish.

With specific regard to children's behavior, the doctor-style parent's weakness, in addition to being obsessed with getting an answer, is often a lack of action, a lack of affection, and a reliance on words to convey feelings. This comes across to a child as an uncaring, aloof attitude. Where the child-style parent and child might stage a joyous celebration if the child brought home a B+ report card, the doctor-style parent's tendency would be to ask, "Why weren't you able to get an A? After all, B+ is so close."

Doctor-Style Fallout: A Cold, Clinical Approach

The fallout seen in doctor-style parent settings is a child's frequent feeling that his or her home life is devoid of emotion. "Children's behavior has a logical, possibly hereditary cause, and explanations for that behavior can be found" expresses the doctor-style parent's view.

Behavior problems stem from the child's frustration (mild or intense) at dealing with "very adult" people. In this respect, children of doctor-style parents often feel pressured into acting like little adults; the greatest put-down for them is being told that their behavior is immature.

In school, any attempt to enforce rules or disciplinary action brings great resistance from these children—"My father won't

be happy to hear about this" (implying that Father's unhappiness
will be directed at the school rather than at Junior). Junior is
used to rapping with Mom or Dad and never really has to come
to grips with his misbehavior. He has learned that simply admitting he is at fault is sufficient to get him off the hook. Say, for
example, that Junior has been involved in some petty theft in the
neighborhood, and his father has found out. He asks his son,
"Why did you do it, Son?" "Well, Dad, it was a case of getting
into bad company [diagnosis], and, believe me, I know I blew it!"
"Good, Son, I hope you've learned a lesson." (Prognosis established.) The doctor-style father is secretly afraid to confront the
misbehavior, fearing a loss of communication.

The father's reaction is a demonstration of a lack of real caring. Although limits are set for the child, they can be bent or
broken, depending on the situation. For example, Junior knows
the limits, but he also knows that if he can concoct convincing-
enough extenuating circumstances, he can be let off the hook. He
knows what Father wants; he gives Father what Father wants.
How does Junior know this? Because doctor-style Father keeps
asking why until Junior hits upon the right reason or excuse for
his misbehavior. This is an exact opposite from the kind of parent who wants no excuses: "All I know is that you broke the
rule—no ifs, ands, or buts—case closed." If anything, the doctor-
style parent and child keep the jury out until a comfortable ver-
dict has been reached.

4

The
Diplomat-Style
Parent

*An appeaser is one who feeds a crocodile—hoping it will
eat him last.*

—Sir Winston Churchill

*This is what is hardest: to close the open hand because one
loves.*

—Friedrich Nietzsche

Diplomat-Style Parents: Ed and Rita Martinelli

Ed and Rita Martinelli have a problem child on their hands.
Mark is now twelve, and, in short, he's gotten just about anything he's ever wanted. The problem is that Ed and Rita are now
faced with Mark's latest demands for new ski equipment, and

since Ed has just lost his job as a writer for a major newspaper, money is very tight.

Both Ed and Rita grew up in lower-middle-class families in Boston, and both felt deprived as children. When they met fifteen years ago, part of their first date was spent discussing their vow that if they ever had children, those children would never suffer the deprivation they had suffered.

If anything, they have been too successful in carrying out their wishes with their only child, Mark.

Both parents know that if Mark doesn't get what he wants, life will be hell for the three of them. Ed has told Rita, "Let's get him the lousy ski equipment. It's better than hearing him complain for the next month." Rita agrees. Remembering that she never had so much as a ski jacket when she was young, she decides, "It's the least we can do," also happy they've avoided Mark's whining. Ed and Rita are diplomat-style parents.

A Diplomat-Style Parent: Jean Thornton

Jean Thornton is a single parent. She and her husband, Ray, divorced three years ago when their son, Terry, was three years old. Since then, Jean has had to work full time to support herself and her son. Ray, unemployed and—to the best of Jean's knowledge—still alcoholic, sends no child-support money, despite the custody agreement.

Terry, a bright, active, and handsome six-year-old boy, has been in the first grade for several months, and, to Jean's great distress, his behavior in school has been horrendous. At times, the child needs to be segregated from the rest of the class because of fits of temper; he throws tantrums when he's told to do something he doesn't want to do. At the first parent-teacher conference, the teacher told Jean about the limits placed on Terry in class and about the rules she had struggled to enforce. Since Terry's behavior seemed to worsen as time went on, the teacher arranged a meeting for Jean with the school psychologist.

Dr. Stevens, who had observed Terry on a day-to-day basis in the classroom, did a psychological workup on Terry, with Jean's permission. He found nothing wrong with the child, and, in his conference following the workup, he counseled Jean on managing her home situation with Terry differently.

Jean told the psychologist that in the three years since her divorce, she has consciously tried to make it up to Terry by providing him with just about anything he asks for. She feels, at times, that she is "raising a monster or a dictator—I can't tell which." When Dr. Stevens asked about her personal life, she poured out a story of Terry's angry reactions to the men she had dated since her divorce, making it almost impossible for her to see the same man more than two or three times. She said she knows Terry needs to be reassured of her love for him, but she feels as if he were running—and ruining—her life. The boy interrupts most conversations she has with visitors (male or female), whining and pulling at her slacks to get her attention. She told Dr. Stevens that she is afraid to be firm with Terry; she never even raises her voice, since, as she put it, "he's only a child."

In order to get Terry to stay with a baby-sitter for a few hours, Jean has to promise him surprises and gifts that are getting more and more expensive. She tries to treat Terry "like a person; we have talks all the time about respecting other people's rights, but they just don't work. He actually behaves well in school compared with the way he is at home."

In fact, when Dr. Stevens suggested the name of an excellent family therapist for Jean and Terry to see, Terry told Jean, "I'm not going. I'll only go if . . ."

Jean is a diplomat-style parent.

What's a Diplomat-Style Parent?

The diplomat-style parent is guided by what the child wants rather than by an adult sense of what the child needs. The diplomat-style parent shuns the role of authority figure and, when confronted by his or her child, seeks the path of least resistance. And, frequently, that path is the precise path desired by the child.

Does that mean that the diplomat-style parent is manipulated, controlled by the child? You bet it does! The child learns very quickly that his or her wishes, opinions, wants, and desires are paramount and that they will be acted upon by the diplomat-style parent.

Remember the term *spoiled brat*? It isn't a very scientific term, but it serves to illustrate the result of a typical diplomat-style parent–child relationship. Just like the joke that asks, "What do you feed a three-hundred-pound canary?" (Answer: "Anything it wants"), the diplomat-style parent gives his or her child just about anything the child wants.

We can understand why a politician or a diplomat might want to reach agreements with other political representatives, but why would a parent want to give in consistently to the demands of a child?

Fear is one reason. Some diplomat-style parents fear their children. They fear that their children will not love them if they don't give them what they want.

Guilt is another reason. Many parents don't like to be the bad guys. It isn't fun for any parent to have to discipline children. There's nothing pleasant about laying down rules and expecting them to be followed. Guilt allows the diplomat-style parent to give in, to appease the child—especially if the parent felt deprived as a child.

Convenience is still another reason. Sometimes it's easier to give in to get what we want—peace and quiet.

Finally, diplomat-style parents are often motivated by love. The internal message is "He will love me if I do what he wants" or "My daughter will love me if I buy her that toy. I know she doesn't really need it, but what's more important—her love or $10.98?"

The Duke of Windsor, on a visit to the United States in 1957, remarked, "The thing that amazes me most about America is the way parents obey their children." Diplomat-style parents do indeed obey their children.

Consider this classic situation involving young children. Two children are arguing over a toy they both want. Here's what three parents, with different parent-styles, would do. The child-style parent would take sides in the dispute, acting like a protective older brother or sister. The doctor-style parent would ask, "Why are you arguing? You guys usually never fight." The diplomat-style parent would seek to resolve the dispute through bribery. The conversation might go something like the following interaction between a four-year-old child and a diplomat-style parent:

CHILD (YELLING):	That's my toy! Give me my toy or I'll hit you! That's my toy!
PARENT (INTERRUPTING):	Jerry, you have had it for a while. Let Johnny play with it now.
CHILD:	No. It's mine and he can't have it!
PARENT (DIPLOMATICALLY):	But we share our toys, don't we?
CHILD:	I don't care. I had it first; it's mine and I want it. (Starts wrestling with Johnny for possession.)
PARENT:	Well, here's what we can do: You give it to Johnny for five minutes and . . .
CHILD (ANGRY):	No!
PARENT (DESPERATELY):	. . . and we'll buy a surprise for you next time we go out!
CHILD:	A surprise? I want a truck! I want a truck!
PARENT (RELIEVED):	Yes, yes. We'll get that truck you saw in K-Mart. Okay?
CHILD (VICTORIOUS):	Here, Johnny. You can have that dumb thing. I'm getting a truck!

In this example, the diplomat-style parent, seeking an immediate peace, bribes the child to get him to behave. Unlike the child-style parent, the diplomat will never argue with kids, preferring to play the role of mediator and, ultimately, appeaser. This leads to the spoiled-brat syndrome, in which the more that's given, the less it's appreciated. Like a snowball rolled down a mountain, this "gimme" thinking on the part of a child is permitted to grow and grow, gathering momentum as time passes.

In her 1945 study of the ways parents relate to their children, Lafore referred to parents who are "appeasers," whose approach is mainly conciliatory. These parents operate under the assumption that giving in is better than battling it out. The appeaser wants to avoid an issue, not to face it at all if possible. How many times have we heard diplomat-style parents pass this philosophy on to their children: "Give it to him so he'll be quiet!"

Diplomat-Style Fallout: "Peace in Our Time"

Of all parent-styles, only the diplomat uses bribes to perfection. And when bribes are used, it's the child who controls the parent—not vice versa. Bribes get results, but they're extremely poor devices for teaching children good behavior. The child does the right thing, but for the wrong reason. The teenage child whose parent offers him or her a bribe to clean up his or her room will probably do so (if the bribe is attractive), but not for the right reason—a sense of personal responsibility. Another hazard of bribery is that the payoff has to get bigger and bigger to maintain its effectiveness.

Children of diplomat-style parents may have a great deal of difficulty functioning in school. Often they demand individual attention, not for learning purposes but simply to get attention. Such children will generally have difficulty in obeying rules, since they are used to a bargaining or negotiating interchange between adult and child. Consider the following example. Bobby, the son of diplomat-style parents, takes a pencil from another child. Rather than giving it back when his classmate discovers it's missing, Bobby negotiates with the teacher: "But I don't have a pencil of my own, and Charley had ten. Can you imagine? He's got ten pencils, and he's complaining about missing one. Here— take your cheap pencil." Bobby is shocked by the reprimand from the teacher that follows. "I gave him his pencil back, didn't I? What more do you want me to do?"

Diplomat-style parents can give rise to one of the most frightening contemporary phenomena—the child tyrant, whose parents are at times little more than slaves to the child. Just as the child-style parent feels powerless, thus giving the child an opportunity to gain control, the diplomat-style parent fears power and comes across to the child as being afraid of him or her. The diplomat-style parent doesn't feel powerless but avoids at all costs using the power he or she has in hand.

The child soon learns that he or she can manipulate the parent. Since the diplomat-style parent is often willing to give in, the child learns not only how to use the parent but also how hard he or she needs to push in order to achieve the desired result. Attributing this scheming characteristic to children might seem strange, but it's important to remember that children learn this behavior from parents.

This point was well made by Edward Ford and Steven Englund in *For the Love of Children*: "Children learn . . . from the people closest to them: their parents . . . the important thing for parents to remember is this: the example you set by your behaviour, not your sermons, is your most important contribution to your child's learning process."

The parent-to-child contact is the child's first contact with the world. Since the child learns how to manipulate the parent, it is reasonable to expect that the child will come to manipulate others in his or her young world.

For example, when the child learns that the parent will eventually give in (and not uphold the rules that have been established), he or she then generalizes that manipulative behavior—expecting teachers, for example, to reward correct schoolwork.

I can give no better example than one from my experience as a teacher. Joan, in my sixth-grade class, was being punished for misbehaving in class. As punishment, she forfeited part of her recess time. In addition to misbehaving, Joan had not done her reading work and had "forgotten" to do last night's mathematics homework. Since she had to stay in anyway, I suggested that she try to finish some of her missed math homework. Her answer? "If I do it, will you let me go outside?" Joan attempted to get a payoff for doing her work—work that was not only overdue but had also been part of her responsibility last night. In addition, she attempted to confuse the fact that she had forfeited part of her recess because of her misbehavior, not because of missing homework.

Passive resistance is another manipulative technique that children can use to control diplomat-style adults. Passive resistance means that the child is uncooperative, but in a meek or passive manner—like the girl who keeps "forgetting" her homework, or the boy who constantly "forgets" to do his household jobs. Children know it's easier for an adult to tell them what to do than it is to get them to do it. At home, this behavior is often unwittingly encouraged by a parent who wants a child to approve of his or her decisions. The child of a diplomat-style parent is an expert when it comes to getting and keeping control of the parent. No other child seems to be so well taught.

5

The Autocrat-Style Parent

We thought, because we had power, we had wisdom.

—Stephen Vincent Benét

An Autocrat-Style Parent: Ralph Carlson

Ralph Carlson has just returned from his daughter's wedding. She did look beautiful, he has to admit. Anger and embarrassment aside, Ralph feels puzzled that Cathy "had" to get married. Sure, he figured that his daughter would be married someday, but this way?

Ralph was very firm with Cathy. He lived through the Depression and World War II and knew hardship. He and Cathy had violent arguments, traceable, perhaps, to the generation gap of the 1970s.

53

Never hesitant about punishment, Ralph was one to act first, talk later because he was certain that when the child had done wrong, the time for talking was over. He expected Cathy to abide by the rules of the house and, more than once, told her that "if you don't like it, there's the door." Ralph also intimidated his wife, who would not dare contradict him in front of *his* children. Ralph wonders how his son and younger daughter will turn out. He longs for the good old days, when children respected their elders and wouldn't think of disgracing their parents. Ralph is an autocrat-style parent.

Autocrat-Style Parents: Stan and Mary Bissel

Stan and Mary Bissel took custody of Stan's nephew Greg when Stan's brother and his wife divorced. Stan's brother is stationed in Japan, and his ex-wife's whereabouts are unknown. Although Greg's mother and father did not get along at all, they often showered him with little gifts to try to win his love. Now that Stan and Mary are in charge, they're going to change that kind of nonsensical behavior toward a child.

The first few months Greg lived with his new parents, there were constant battles of will between Greg and Stan. First of all, Stan felt he had to teach Greg how to act like a man. Allowed to play with dolls and stuffed animals when he lived with his natural parents, Greg had to give them up when Stan ordered them thrown away. "Let him play with normal boys' toys," he told his wife. Greg's protests were dealt with sternly.

When Greg was seven years old, Mary insisted that he spend less time reading and more time helping to do work outside the house and in the garage. Greg misses his parents terribly and dreams of running away from Stan and Mary. Once, when he tried, Stan came after him and beat him, calling him a spoiled brat and a sissy. An investigation is under way to reassign custody, begun by Greg's other uncle, who wants to give him a better home. Stan and Mary insist that all Greg needs is a home like theirs, with "firm morals and structure." Stan and Mary are autocrat-style parents.

What's an Autocrat-Style Parent?

The autocrat-style parent's favorite adage could well be "Spare the rod and spoil the child." Given this attitude, it's not hard to understand why the autocrat-style parent seemingly has the best-behaved children in town. Unfortunately, such good behavior is not likely to be the healthy, well-adjusted behavior most parents would like to instill in their children.

Probably more has been written about this authoritarian personality than about any other style, due to the sometimes extreme antidemocratic nature of such parents' modus operandi. Autocrat-style parents present problems for teachers, principals, and others who must deal with them. Such parents are often the ones who demand that more homework be assigned, disparage new teaching and learning techniques, question the need for individualized instruction in the classroom, and, in general, wonder why things can't be as they were in the good old days.

The autocrat-style parent is an order giver at home, the opposite of the classical democratic parent and the permissive parent. Often, the child of an autocrat-style parent has little chance to feel that his or her thoughts and wishes count. One of the most severe consequences of this is that since the child is never given responsibility to make his or her own decisions, he or she grows up literally unable to think for himself or herself.

The autocrat-style parent is not more commonly Father, despite stereotypes to that effect. The odds are that Mother and Father are both autocrat-style parents. The recent trend toward more democratic marriages has not affected the autocrat-style parent at all. As one parent told me at a school conference, he found a "good wife . . . despite all the 'libbers' out there."

The chances for healthy adjustment in the child are not great if this style is extreme. Children of autocrat-style parents sometimes have difficulty adjusting to school, especially to schools where they're not given constant direction and where there aren't "old-fashioned" teachers who teach with a hick'ry stick. A Montessori school or an open classroom is probably not the place where a child of autocrat-style parents can even hope to function successfully. It's a vicious circle. The open classroom concept would probably be scorned by the parent, thus reducing the chances for the child's success in such a setting even more.

The autocrat-style parent can be characterized by his or her "because I told you so" attitude when speaking.

PARENT: Clean your room.

CHILD: Why do I have to?

PARENT: Because I told you to do it.

CHILD: It's not fair. Suzie didn't clean her room.

PARENT: I'm not talking to Suzie. I told you to do it, so do it!

Autocrat-Style Fallout: "Do Nothing Until You Hear from Me"

So used to being told what to do, the child of autocrat-style parents is often incapable of making sound, constructive, and beneficial decisions that affect his or her life. Such children are often seen as well behaved, quiet, and obedient—descriptions on which their parents pride themselves.

Sex adjustment is sometimes difficult for children of autocrat-style parents. Emphasis is not placed on sex itself but on sex roles. Boys are expected to act "like boys," and girls are expected to act "like girls." There are strong prohibitions in the autocrat-style family against, for example, boys showing the slightest interest in playing with dolls, or in girls wanting to play football. It makes life confusing for the child, since there's no apparent reason why footballs are sometimes great (Super Bowl Sunday) and dolls sometimes forbidden (when played with by the "wrong" sex).

Because the parent often views education and creativity with suspicion, the child comes to see them as being of dubious value.

Generally, too, the child of an autocrat-style parent is encouraged not to express feelings—to be timid or shy—and is constantly seeking to get and keep the parent's approval. Such children are highly concerned with a right and a wrong way to act and often express this concern. "It's wrong for boys to cry." "It's wrong for women to wear pants. How silly! Men wear pants." Unfortunately, this notion of right and wrong is more commonly tied to social convention (sex stereotypes or what-will-the-neighbors-think ideals) than to morality.

Children of autocrat-style parents often do not have insight into their behavior. Where the doctor-style and the diplomat-style parents rely to a great degree on talking and communicating, the autocrat-style parent often dismisses an issue with "There's nothing to talk about. You did the wrong thing, and that's all there is to say"—thus giving the child little opportunity to reflect on his or her behavior.

The autocrat-style parent instills in his or her child a sense of safety in obedience. Certainly, obedience is important, but the degree to which obedience is sought is of questionable value. The crucial choices the child will have to make when he or she grows older will require independent thinking—not blind adherence to rules.

6

The Martyr-Style Parent

Martyrs, my friend, have to choose between being forgotten, mocked or used. As for being understood— never.

—Albert Camus

A Martyr-Style Parent: Jane Martin

As Jane Martin returns home from work, that familiar feeling in the pit of her stomach develops as she approaches her apartment. As soon as she walks in, the dirty kitchen floor and the sink full of dishes greet her. She makes a mental note to get to them as soon as she can—as soon as she can start supper, as soon as she can find a clean saucepan, as soon as she can put away the groceries. And the cat's litter box is overflowing. Jane's oldest son, Jeff, a high school senior, tells her that he'll have to miss supper—he's on his way to the library to do research for a report due tomorrow.

Eric, her seventh-grader, is in a foul mood, and he refuses to help Jane with dinner or the housework. Frustrated, Jane unplugs his television set, but, as in the past, it does no good. Eric goes to his bedroom, more angry than before and determined not to give in and do "girl's housework." He dreams of having Jeff's freedom and resents the "favored" treatment Jeff enjoys. (Actually, Jeff has threatened to leave his mother and Eric to live with his father.) When Eric comes out of his room, a screaming session begins over television, school, helping around the house, and many other older hurts. Nothing is resolved. When Jeff returns from the library two hours later, he goes to his room to finish his assignment. He can't work at the kitchen table, where Jane sits, in tears, silently chain-smoking as she wonders what she did to deserve this life. Jane is well educated and has a lucrative position at the bank. But she operates as a martyr-style parent.

A Martyr-Style Parent: Don Vega

Don, a youngish-looking forty years old, is on his way to school for an urgent conference with his daughter's teacher. Cindy has been having some serious problems with her temper. She came close to striking her sixth-grade teacher after hurling some choice words at her. This scene has happened before.

Don's own parents were strict, puritanical, upstanding citizens who were totally out of touch with his feelings as a growing child, and Don's lifelong ambition as a parent is to be the kind of father he never had. In the past, when Don has been called to school over less serious offenses, he has tried behavior modification, promising Cindy a reward if her behavior improves. Indeed, she got a new bicycle after last term's conference, and her teacher said that her behavior changed for the better—at least for five days.

This time, however, Don wonders what he could have done (or

not have done) to cause Cindy's most recent outburst. Even before he sits down with Mr. Markwell, Don admits, "I don't know
what I'm doing wrong with Cindy. I know I'm not the best parent
there is—I just don't know what to do with her." Mr. Markwell
advises Don to be firmer with Cindy, to rely less on rewards for
one or two days of good behavior, and he offers to set up a daily
home-school communication letter. But he may just as well advise Don to fly to the moon, since there's little likelihood that
Don will follow Mr. Markwell's advice, feeling that Cindy's problems are a result of his inadequacy as a parent. Don means well;
he loves Cindy deeply. But Don—like Jane Martin—operates as
a martyr-style parent.

What's a Martyr-Style Parent?

In this era of "me first" parenting, the martyr-style's slogan is
"my fault" parenting. The essence is "I" or "me"; usually it's
"Why me?" or "What did I do to deserve this?"

The martyr-style parent sees himself or herself as the cause
behind a misbehaving child or a household that doesn't run
smoothly. And, as was the case with Don, the parent confuses
rewards with bribes, mischief with misbehavior. He or she has
difficulty teaching the child to respect others because, due to his
or her own lack of self-esteem, the parent has never demanded
respect.

No parent-style is more prone to use guilt effectively than the
martyr-style parent. My friend's mother often said to her son,
"When I die, don't come crying to my funeral, saying 'I wish I
had listened to her.'" Now *that* is guilt.

As is true with other parent-styles, the relationship between
the martyr-style parent and his or her children can be a vicious
circle. The parent's feeling that he or she is unworthy of another
person's respect gets through loud and clear to the child. Disrespect (and disobedience) follow, which the martyr-style parent
accepts as his or her just deserts, since, the reasoning goes, he or
she is not worth respect in the first place. Rodney Dangerfield,

the comedian, speaks for many parents when he laments, "I get no respect . . . no respect at all."

Where I live, no bus service is provided for high school students. Thus, arrangements for driving the children to school are made among the parents. Lee, one of the mothers who is involved in the car pool, was complaining to me about three of the seven children she drives. "They're always late. Sometimes five minutes, sometimes ten or fifteen minutes late. That's the reason why I'm late for work after dropping the kids off."

I asked Lee if she'd spoken to the teenagers; they'd certainly understand, I said.

"Spoken to them? Only five or six times, Bob!"

I told Lee to speak up once more. Tell the riders that she was leaving at 7:15 sharp starting Monday morning and that she was serious about it. Lee felt bad about doing this.

"I don't want them to miss school. It would be twenty miles for them to hitchhike, and if something happened to them, I'd never forgive myself."

Lee didn't realize it, but she was a true martyr-style victim. Each morning she made the decision to wait for those late children, despite the fact that she knew that she'd be late for work as a result. When I asked a few more questions, I realized that Lee didn't want to antagonize the late riders, fearing they'd retaliate by excluding her daughters from the high school clique. Lee thought she was sacrificing herself for her daughters' welfare. She was carrying her generosity and self-sacrifice to a point where it became self-punishment.

To take it one step further, Lee was probably taking the easy way out. Martyr-style parents sometimes use an escape technique to avoid a confrontation, to avoid unpleasantness, and, most of all, to avoid having their children think badly of them. Ironically, Lee did not realize that what was better for her (getting to work on time) was also better for the children. It was an opportunity for them to learn the value of promptness, courtesy, consideration, and caring in human relationships.

Martyr-Style Fallout: "God, Give Me Strength"

The greatest goal in life for a child of a martyr-style parent is to tune out all the complaints, the guilt, the unhappiness, and, somehow, to rise above it all. Like the diplomat-style parent, the martyr-style parent wants a harmonious relationship with the child. The martyr-style parent will go a step further than the diplomat, however, by putting his or her head on the block, if necessary, to secure that peace. In the martyr-style scheme of things, the child owes a great debt to the parent, one that can never be repaid. The parent is seen as weak, and that sets the stage for tremendous resentment by the child.

Breaking a rule causes more anguish for the parent than it does for the child. Although no real punishment is meted out, a heavy guilt trip—"Now see what you've done to me"—is laid like a granite cornerstone. Misbehavior is taken personally by the martyr-style parent (the opposite of the doctor-style parent's attitude); and emotions, tears, and sometimes near hysterics are involved. It's not a healthy situation, especially when extreme.

As might be expected, the child of the martyr-style parent becomes skillful at avoiding behavior that might cause such a scene. He or she tends not to take chances or to be different. The child does what he or she is told to do in school, not because the child fears punishment or thinks that not to obey would be wrong (as is the case with the child of autocrat-style parents), but because the child doesn't want to punish the martyr that he or she knows as Mom or Dad.

Martyr-style parents who use guilt to control and dominate children to get them to do what the parent wants are called dominant martyr-style parents.

Sometimes, however, the child of martyr-style parents manages to use his or her parent's weakness to excellent advantage. Depending on how much the parent sacrifices for the child, there may be a situation in which the child is in control. We could call this the submissive martyr-style—the child can throw back the guilt on the parent. In such a case, the child might take advantage of the parent, as in this example: "I want new skates . . . I want new skis . . . I want a new car." "No? . . . Don't you love me?"

The submissive martyr-style parent is often willing to take the blame for the child's failings in life, feeling that it was his or her fault for bringing the child into the world. ("It's all your fault, Mom. I never asked to be born.") The martyr-style parent can find protecting the child to be counterproductive. For example, if the parent writes a note to the teacher that says, "It's my fault Donald was late—I didn't set his alarm clock," the parent is letting the child off the hook with no consequences or, at least, reduced consequences.

One of the undesirable fallout effects of the dominant martyr-style is its tendency to encourage children not to take chances or to be different. "When you're bad, it hurts Mommy." With that message (powerful guilt), the child is too fearful of hurting his or her parent, and if the child should misbehave, the martyr cycle continues: "It's my fault, Mommy, that you're hurt."

7

The Talker-Style Parent

We promise much to avoid giving little.

—Marquis de Vauvenargues

Talkers are no good doers.

—Shakespeare

A Talker-Style Parent: Rose Levitt

"Nag, nag, nag—Mom, that's all you ever do. When I have a problem, do you try to help me? No. You tell me you love me and want me to be happy, but don't you realize that you cause much of my unhappiness? If you'd only be quiet and listen for a change, that would be different. If you think you can bring up my kids better than I can, you're wrong. You had your chance to be a parent; now let me have mine. Stop nagging me all the time."

With that, Dave Levitt ended a visit at his mother's house. When he returned home, he told his wife about his conversation with Mother. "She knows what's best for me—or so she says. How in God's name can I go back to college? She thinks she knows everything. Who will pay the bills if I go back to school? What will you and the kids do—eat at her house every night? She'd like that."

Dave, who has two young children of his own, has been battling his mother for twenty-two years—since he was born. His father worked seven days a week and was not involved in the "discussions" between Dave and his mother. His mother's refrain was that Dave never listened to her and would wind up a bum. Dave resented her nagging, and he's glad to be living away from her now. Dave's mother, Rose Levitt, is a talker-style parent.

A Talker-Style Parent: Marcia Norman

Marcia Norman was happiest when her daughter, Joyce, was a baby. Each day brought happy times for baby and mother. Since Marcia had lost two babies in delivery before Joyce was born, her relationship to Joyce was very protective.

Since Joyce started junior high school, it hasn't been smooth sailing for her and Marcia. Marcia feels that Joyce is getting in with the "wrong crowd," and that her daughter has tuned her out. Joyce wishes her mother would "stop nagging" and listen to her for a change, and her mother reminisces about the past, when the two of them would play together those silly, wonderful baby-mother games. Marcia is afraid of losing her daughter to bad influence, and her words and long lectures seem to fall on deaf ears. Marcia is a talker-style parent.

What's a Talker-Style Parent?

"My child never seems to listen to me. I think he's hard of hearing," said one parent to me at a conference. After I'd listened to her nonstop chatter for a half hour, she observed, "I haven't given you a chance to speak, have I?" She had told me—in a half hour—her son's history, complete with excuses for his trouble with math (she was poor in math as a student—aha!). She went on to say that he's really a good boy who takes the blame unfairly in the classroom. During a half-hour conversation, Mrs. Verbose stopped only once—to comment on her behavior—and then picked up again where she had left off.

The talker is a common parent-style, and it's one of the more difficult ones to overcome. Since the talker-style parent tends to be nonanalytical and often seeks excuses for misbehavior, he or she may fail to see the negative effects of this style. The talker-style parent literally talks himself or herself out of finding a way to make a significant change in the home situation. A Catch-22 situation develops, where the more the talker-style parent talks, the less he or she is listened to. "My predominant style is talker, but I really don't think I am . . . I think that people kind of tune me out . . . it's not my fault." Talker-style parents, beware!

You can observe a classical talker-style parent in action at a Laundromat. Just keep an eye out for a child—or children—wildly careening on the tiled floor. You may not be able to tell who the parent is by looking, but if you listen carefully, there will be one adult who will occasionally turn and yell something at the child that has absolutely no effect on him or her. The "Laundromat child" is a master at tuning out his or her parent—with good reason, I suppose.

An interaction between a talker-style parent and his or her child might go something like this—a variation on the "my child never listens" theme.

PARENT: Pick up those clothes! I spend good money for clothing, and money doesn't grow on trees. How many times do I have to tell you? Over and over again. I'm sick of repeating, and . . .

CHILD: Huh?

PARENT: . . . I never have to tell your sister because she's neat . . . if those clothes are on the floor, you won't go out . . . if those toys aren't picked up, I'm going to . . .

CHILD: Okay, okay! (Turn if off—please!)

Generally, the talker-style parent does not want to fight or argue. If anything, this parent wants peacefulness and cares deeply for children. When the child does indeed tune out, the parent will talk more, instead of evaluating the effect of his or her words and trying a less verbose approach.

If directly confronted, the talker-style parent will sometimes back off from an argument, adopting a martyr-style stance: "Why are you getting angry at me? I was only trying to help you!"

As might be expected, the talker-style parent is almost powerless in changing children's behavior for any length of time. Here's one last example. Three parents are sitting around a table, having a cup of coffee—their children playing in the other room. A loud quarrel breaks out among the children. One of the parents, a talker-style, stops her adult conversation, yells something at the child(ren), and then resumes her adult conversation, saying something like "Never a moment's peace with that boy of mine!" Thus, with a smile, the talker-style parent has dished out her brand of behavior improvement. It rarely works, and if it does, it doesn't last very long.

The talker-style parent has little effect on children's behavior. His or her habitual chatter can lead to frustration for both parent and child.

Talker-Style Fallout: "I Won't Listen Unless You'll Be Quiet"

Schools, with their emphasis on verbal communication—someone's usually talking, and someone's usually listening—present special problems for the child of talker-style parents. When someone's talking (such as the teacher), the talker-style child often has difficulty paying attention because he or she has developed an unfailing mechanism for ignoring adult chatter. (Imagine the difficulty when the child has a talker-style teacher.)

In addition to difficulties with listening and paying attention, the child may also have difficulty in expressing himself or herself because, odds are, the child's speech patterns have been shaped by years of trying, and failing, to find a receptive ear at home.

This presents a problem when children of talker-style parents attempt to deal with friends, because the verbal communication patterns these children have practiced at home are not likely to win them a flock of devoted friends. These children are probably not shy and passive; they may be big shots, big mouths, or bullies. Other children fear—or, more likely, dislike—this behavior and tend to avoid playmates who display it.

Like the child of martyr-style and diplomat-style parents, the child of talker-style parents may expect a payoff in money, attention, or material goods for behaving well. The child will see these objects—especially money and material goods—as signs of love and will attach an importance to them beyond their real value. Unfortunately, bribes work well with talker-style children. Reasoning does not work at all.

Seldom does the child of a talker-style parent have to account for his or her own behavior. Since the child is let off easily at home, he or she assumes that if you do something wrong, you probably won't have to pay for it or suffer the consequences. A parent who can always be counted on to defend his or her child is usually only trying to be protective but is, in effect, teaching the child that "Mommy or Daddy will bail you out."

When communication is not effective (as in the relationship between the talker-parent and his or her child), other kinds of undesirable behavior crop up. For example, when the talker-style parent rambles on and on—instead of making the discussion short and to the point—he or she creates a frustrating situation for the child. And that frustration may be translated into "fresh" responses and rude behavior.

8
Identifying
Your
Parent-Style

*Parentage is a very important profession; but no test of
fitness for it is ever imposed in the interest of the children.*

—George Bernard Shaw

To help you learn about your parent-style, I have devised a very
simple test that will enable you to identify your predominant
(primary) style and your strong (secondary) style or styles.

In the exercises that follow, you'll find a list of statements for
each of the parent-styles we've discussed. I call these statements
descriptors because they describe characteristics of a particular
style. For each style, there are ten descriptors and a space for
you to score each one.

Taking the Test

As you read each descriptor, consider how accurately it describes your behavior or feelings as a parent or how accurately it represents your viewpoint toward raising children.

Give yourself three points for each descriptor that accurately describes your feelings or actions as a parent.

Give yourself two points for each descriptor that is sometimes accurate or partly accurate.

Give yourself one point for each descriptor that is rarely or never accurate.

Mark your choices (1, 2, or 3) on the blank line next to the appropriate descriptor.

For each style, you should have ten scores. Add the scores and write the total in the space provided.

There is only one rule: You must be honest. Do not confuse the kind of parent you think is ideal with your actual behavior or feelings. Answer the way that most accurately describes your true behavior or viewpoint—not the way you wish you were. As you consider each descriptor, try to picture yourself in typical, day-to-day situations with your children. Leave no descriptor unanswered.

Take as much time as you need. Work on this test when you have some quiet time for yourself. Consider each statement carefully, but don't hesitate to put down your first reaction—sometimes those first reactions are the most accurate.

DESCRIPTORS: THE CHILD-STYLE PARENT

YOU:

1. Can set standards of acceptable behavior for children but have difficulty enforcing them. _____

2. Feel like a victim—not in control of your life. _____

3. Believe that love is the most important ingredient in teaching good behavior. _____

4. Dislike hearing children say, "You're not being fair!" _____

5. Think that children's feelings are more important than their actions. _____

6. Have a strong sense of honesty. _____

7. Seek your child's approval for decisions that would affect him or her. _____

8. Prefer—for your child—happiness over riches, friendship over fame. _____

9. Share your child's sense of humor. _____

10. Would rather give one more chance than punish when confronted with a behavior problem. _____

TOTAL _____

DESCRIPTORS: THE DOCTOR-STYLE PARENT

YOU:

1. Think that there's an answer for a child's misbehavior, that there's a reason why children misbehave. _____

2. Find children illogical. _____

3. Think that the world is structured and well organized, that problems have solutions. _____

4. Contact other adults or professionals, if necessary, to find a solution to a behavior problem. _____

5. Want very much to be the ideal parent. _____

6. Feel that a good talk can improve behavior, that misbehavior is caused by a lack of communication. _____

7. Prefer the company of adults if given a choice between adults and children. _____

8. Ask yourself or the child why when the child misbehaves. _____

9. Avoid physical punishment, even for serious rule breaking, etc. _____

10. Hate to baby-sit. _____

TOTAL _____

DESCRIPTORS: THE DIPLOMAT-STYLE PARENT

YOU:

1. Have a strong sense of fairness. _____

2. Want your child to approve of your decisions. _____

3. Do not argue with children. _____

4. Are essentially an honest person but might lie or varnish the facts to save a child's feelings. _____

5. Feel that your child often gets his or her way. _____

6. Will use bribes with children. _____

7. Believe that a lack of communication is the main cause of most behavior problems. _____

8. Will give in, even if you know you're right. _____

9. Generally do what your child wants you to do. _____

10. Do not believe in spanking—ever. _____

TOTAL _____

DESCRIPTORS: THE AUTOCRAT-STYLE PARENT
YOU:

1. Feel that children are worse behaved today than when you were young. _____

2. Expect boys to act like boys, and girls to act like girls. _____

3. Feel that parents should be in complete control of their children's behavior. _____

4. Believe that actions speak louder than words, that talking to children about their behavior doesn't usually do much good. _____

5. Believe that physical work is more worthwhile than mental work. _____

6. Don't like to admit you're wrong. _____

7. Can dole out punishment without feeling uncertain, guilty, or doubtful. You know what has to be done, and you rely on no one else but yourself to do it. _____

8. Obey rules, and you expect the same of children. _____

9. Are sometimes suspicious of educated people. _____

10. Feel that there's good behavior and there's bad behavior—nothing in between. _____

TOTAL _____

DESCRIPTORS: THE MARTYR-STYLE PARENT

YOU:

1. Are a sensitive and loving parent—give of yourself at all times. _____

2. Want a harmonious relationship with your child, even if it means personal hardship. _____

3. Have a low opinion of your ability as a parent. _____

4. Are willing to sacrifice your personal needs to provide for children's needs. _____

5. Feel that no one listens to you. _____

6. Use guilt to control children's behavior. Use phrases like "Now see what you've done to me," "No matter what I do, you're never satisfied," "You hurt me because you did that." _____

7. Are usually willing to take the blame for your child's misbehavior or failings. _____

8. Want to be the ideal parent but have no idea how to become one. _____

9. Encourage children not to take chances, to play it safe by not being different. _____

10. Feel helpless as a parent. _____

TOTAL _____

DESCRIPTORS: THE TALKER-STYLE PARENT

YOU:

1. Get tired of hearing yourself talk.   ———

2. Feel that you're tuned out, that children don't listen to you.   ———

3. Care deeply for children and shower them with praise.   ———

4. Defend your child, no matter what.   ———

5. Feel that the world is tough enough, that you don't want to add to it by being strict with children.   ———

6. Are generous with money and material things.   ———

7. Will lie to save a child's feelings or reputation.   ———

8. Feel that there are things you've said a hundred times to children.   ———

9. Make excuses for misbehavior (for example, "His father was like that," "He takes after me," "That teacher must have it in for you—she's always picking on you").   ———

10. Prefer the company of babies to older children.   ———

             TOTAL ———

Scoring the Test

Now that you have completed each of the descriptors, use the scorecard below to record your totals.

Write each of your totals in column 1 below, next to the corresponding parent-style. If, for example, your total score for the ten child-style descriptors was 21, write 21 in column 1, next to "Child." Leave column 2 and column 3 blank for now.

SCORECARD

Parent-Style	Column 1 TOTALS	Column 2 McDonald's Test	Column 3 GRAND TOTALS
CHILD			
DOCTOR			
DIPLOMAT			
AUTOCRAT			
MARTYR			
TALKER			

You are now ready for the second and final part of the test: the "McDonald's Test."

Most parents have probably taken their children to a McDonald's restaurant for quick service and delicious food. The reason why I've called this part of the test the McDonald's Test is not only because most of us have been to McDonald's but also because it's a good setting for observing the six different parent-styles. Here's how it works.

John and Sally Whosis are leaving McDonald's with their son Custer. Little Cuss, like most children, is sometimes temperamental, and this is one of those times. He wants a box of cookies. His mother, Sally Whosis, says, "No, Custer, you've had enough to eat." Dear little Cuss is not satisfied with the answer; so, just before they get to the exit, Custer insists.

Here are some possible responses:

CHILD-STYLE: Ask your father [or mother].

DOCTOR-STYLE: We'll have to talk about this in the car! [Or, when we get home.]

DIPLOMAT-STYLE: Okay, okay. Get the cookies, but don't ask for anything else.

AUTOCRAT-STYLE: How *dare* you ask for another thing! Get moving . . . now!

MARTYR-STYLE: This is my thanks? This is the way you say thank you for my taking you out? No matter what I do, you're never happy.

TALKER-STYLE: Come on, let's go. I don't think they have any cookies left. Hurry up, they're closing. We can't get any cookies . . . they're old and stale, right? You don't want stale cookies . . . we'll get you good cookies later . . .

Select two of the above responses that you might make. Give yourself five points for the response you'd most likely make, and place a +5 in column 2 across from the appropriate style. Then give yourself three points for the other response you selected, placing a +3 in column 2 across from the appropriate style. Now add these points to the corresponding totals in column 1, and put the grand total (the sum of column 1 + column 2 scores) in column 3.

You're not finished yet.

Now select two response styles from the McDonald's Test that you would definitely not make. Place a −5 in column 2 across from the appropriate style for the response you'd be least likely to make; place a −3 on the appropriate line in column 2 for the other unlikely response. Column 2 should now have four spaces filled and two vacant. Place a zero in the spaces in column 2 that are unfilled. Now subtract the "definitely not" responses in column 2 from the total in column 1. Put the answer in column 3 under "Grand Totals." Fill in the blanks in column 3.

You should have six grand total scores—one for each style of parenting. Now take each grand total score and plot it on the StyleGram.

Since each circle on the StyleGram represents five points, the axes go from 0 to 35. Place a dot or mark on the appropriate axis for each grand total score (from column 3 on the scorecard).

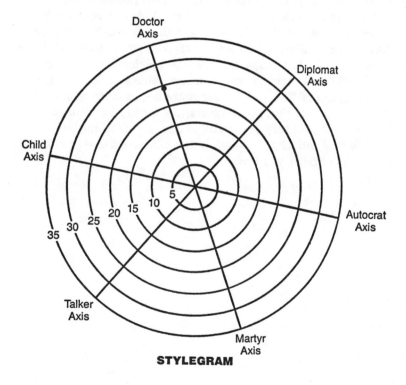

STYLEGRAM

If, for example, your score is a grand total of 24 for the doctor-style, place a dot on the "doctor axis" of the StyleGram. The doctor axis is at the top of the StyleGram. So, in this case, you'd place a dot just before the "25" circle. (A sample dot has been placed there as a reference. Ignore it when recording your true doctor score on the StyleGram.)

The Results

After you've plotted points on each of the six parent-style axes, connect the points to get a clear picture or diagram of your leading styles. The point farthest from the center indicates your predominant style, and the next farthest point (or points) from the center indicates your strong style(s). Your predominant style and your strong style can give you a good idea of your modus operandi as a parent; they can provide valuable insight into your behavior with children. Remember, these styles should not be viewed as labels, handicaps, or personality defects. Rather, they are informal indicators to help you see some of your possible behavior patterns. These style scores are not exact measures of personality, nor are they precise tests, like those administered by a psychologist. But they are useful in providing insight into the ways you deal with children—ways that can have a drastic effect on the lives of those you love.

9

The
Style-Seven
Parent

*Not a having and a resting, but a growing and a becoming,
is the character of perfection. . . .*

—Matthew Arnold

A Style-Seven Parent: Paul Conway

Paul Conway is exhausted—he's just gotten out of his car, and
he's walking slowly toward his house. His day has been very
difficult and frustrating. As soon as he walks in the door, his five-
year-old daughter rushes up to see him, crying, "Daddy! Look
what I did in kindergarten today!" She shows him her drawing of
him as he bends to pick her up and hug her. Despite his fatigue,
he carries her to the couch for their nightly "tickle fight."

As Mrs. Lynch, the baby-sitter, gets ready to leave, Paul says to her, "Everything okay today?" With a smile, Mrs. Lynch says, "Of course. Beth couldn't wait until you got home. Goodnight."

Paul puts away his briefcase and prepares supper. His wife, Marge, usually cooks dinner, but tonight is her late night at work. As Paul and Beth eat supper, Beth tells about the things she did during the day and what she's looking forward to doing tomorrow. Paul listens as Beth talks to him. "Dad, after supper can we go out for a ride or just for a walk?" Paul says, "No, I'm too tired tonight. How about tomorrow night after supper?" "Okay, Dad—great." The next night, Paul's tired, but he doesn't go back on his word.

Next week at the kindergarten parent-teacher conference, Beth's teacher tells Paul and Marge: "Your little Beth never stops talking about you. You must be doing something right! She tells me, 'Did you know my Daddy did this—my Mommy did that?' Beth sure thinks the world of you two."

Although Beth's report card is not perfect, Paul and Marge are happy that she is doing well in school. The comments of Beth's teacher mean more to them than marks on her card. Both Paul and Marge have style-seven qualities.

A Style-Seven Parent: Angela Dawson

Angela Dawson has had a hard life in many respects. She lost her parents in an auto accident twelve years ago, and her first marriage ended in divorce. Her second husband, Jerry, is a laborer, and the Dawsons find it almost impossible to make ends meet. In addition to their own three children, Angela's nephew Eric lives with them. Eric's mother put him up for adoption after she gave birth to him at a home for unwed mothers. When Angela heard about her sister's intentions, she offered to take Eric in until her sister got her life straightened out and wanted him back, or until Eric's mother decided that Angela should adopt him.

Angela is regarded as a great mother and a super parent by the people in town—not just because she is a kind person, but because she seems like one of the few mothers who is deeply respected by her children. In addition to her full-time job as a mother, Angela works as a waitress on weekend nights to help pay some of the bills. She had quite a time convincing Jerry that it's okay for a woman to work. Jerry's values are traditional, but he feels that Angela knows what's best for herself.

Despite her hardships and her occasional concerns that she could be doing a better job as a parent, Angela has many style-seven qualities, and her children (and the neighbors) know it.

What's a Style-Seven Parent?

In deciding what to call this parent-style, I found that many terms that are already in use have lost much of their meaning through overuse or misuse. Besides, there is really no easy way to talk about the kind of parent who has positive attributes from different styles, plus a few more. We've all heard of the good parent, the effective parent, the strong parent, but these terms don't tell us very much. We know that we want to be good parents, but to try to describe one or to try to help people learn how to become one is an impossible task. We've thrown out those overused terms because they don't have any use in our program to help people develop fully as parents. We'll refer instead to the style-seven parent and describe some of his or her qualities.

The style-seven parent is not the perfect parent—far from it. Nor is the style-seven parent the ideal parent. As we did before, let's throw out these words, *perfect* and *ideal,* because they mean nothing. Nobody's perfect; no parent is ideal.

Some of the qualities of the style-seven parent are described below.

Openness. The style-seven parent is open to new ideas, to different ways of approaching behavior problems. He or she is not restricted to "If I told you once, I've told you a thousand times" behavior. Instead, the style-seven parent looks for new paths when the old ones don't work.

A Willingness to Take Risks. The style-seven parent takes

risks—not risks with the health or safety of children but personal risks. He or she is not afraid to step into the unknown, to take a chance by doing something differently.

A Sense of Becoming. The style-seven parent feels let down at times, but he or she knows the satisfaction of personal growth. The style-seven parent feels he or she is not staying put or marking time. The style-seven parent is not one to throw up his or her hands, saying, "I'm doing the best I can," but simply makes the best of his or her role as parent.

Flexibility. The style-seven parent can anticipate behavior. Such a parent can somehow feel the mood, can sense what's going to happen, and can quickly adapt to the situation. He or she does not have standard punishments ("Does this mean no supper, Mom?") to cover different misbehaviors but truly fits the punishment to the crime.

Optimism. The style-seven parent doesn't say things like "John's been a bad boy since he was born—he'll never change," or "Ann's just like me—she has a mean streak and a temper to match." The style-seven parent does not condemn children with a lifetime label—bad temper, lazy, mean streak, can't do math, or similar labels. Instead, there's a happy, optimistic feeling that comes from knowing that if there is a problem, it's being addressed and worked on. When we use labels, it means we've given up. It's easy to say "She's a bad girl"—easier than doing something about it. If a style-seven parent has a child who is having difficulty doing algebra in school, for example, rather than saying "He's bad in math" and giving up, the parent will get additional help for the child, insure that the home situation is conducive to thoughtful, quiet work, and give what time he or she can to help. If the style-seven parent does not have the time to help or doesn't know anything about algebra, he or she will convey the message: "I care. I want you to do well in school. You don't have to be the best, but I won't let you off the hook by saying 'You're bad in math.'" Last, the child of the style-seven parent knows his or her parent cares little about grade level, knows his or her parent neither expects nor cares if he or she is the best in the class, and knows—by his or her parent's words, support, and kindness—that the parent does care about him or her—more than about algebra.

Most importantly, the style-seven parent gives his or her child a *chance to be good*, a chance to make something special out of his or her life. The parent doesn't drag the child to music lessons, drama lessons, and ballet instruction. He or she gives the child an opportunity to pursue areas of interest but does not force them down the child's throat. Nor does the style-seven parent feel compelled to provide activities just because "all the kids are doing it." Some style-seven parents are wealthy; some have difficulty buying shoes for their children. Religion and race don't matter. Style-seven parents come in all shapes and sizes. Giving a child a chance to be good costs nothing and is contrary to no religion. Sure, it takes a little time, patience, and, maybe, adjustment, but the beneficial effects far outweigh the time invested. A chance to be good is a chance for a lifetime—a chance to grow up feeling good about one's self. How much more success could a parent desire?

On the next page is a list of ten descriptors of the style-seven parent. As you have done with the six previous styles, read each descriptor and give yourself three points for each descriptor that accurately describes your feelings or actions as a parent. Give yourself two points for each descriptor that is sometimes accurate or partly accurate. Give yourself one point for each descriptor that is rarely or never accurate. Add the scores to arrive at a total and enter the total in the space provided.

The McDonald's Test Bonus

You saw how John and Sally Whosis had difficulty with their son Custer when Sally said, "No, Custer, you've had enough to eat." Cuss didn't accept Sally's no; he fussed and insisted. Place a zero in the bonus space if this situation occurs or has occurred between you and your child. Place a +5 in the bonus space if your child would have accepted your answer and left the restaurant without a fuss. Add your bonus score to your total to arrive at your style-seven score.

Turn back to the StyleGram. Mark your style-seven score on the StyleGram by placing an X on each of the six axes. For example, if your style-seven score is 30, place an X at the point where *each* axis meets the "30" circle. Connect the Xs (using a different color pen or pencil will help differentiate your Xs from your dots).

DESCRIPTORS: THE STYLE-SEVEN PARENT

YOU:

1. Are not perfect but feel you're becoming a better parent each day. _____

2. Set reasonable limits and standards for acceptable behavior before problems develop. _____

3. Feel no guilt nor sadness when enforcing limits with children. Your child realizes the consequences of breaking rules. _____

4. Are fulfilled by having and raising children, and not by what children do or might do in the future. Live *with* the child, not *through* the child. _____

5. Have a clear idea of how to achieve your own happiness, and you're doing it every day. _____

6. Feel that trying something is more important than being the best at it. _____

7. Have built and maintained a firm bond of love, respect, and kinship with children. You're not merely a pal or friend to your children. _____

8. Praise children's accomplishments in an honest way. _____

9. Can sense or anticipate misbehavior in children. Before it happens, you're aware of it. _____

10. Know that good behavior is learned. You do not feel that misbehavior is inherited—caused by "bad genes" or "faulty chromosomes." You believe firmly that poor behavior can be replaced with appropriate, healthy behavior. _____

TOTAL _____

BONUS _____

STYLE-SEVEN SCORE _____

If your style-seven diagram exceeds each of the other styles on your StyleGram, then style-seven is your predominant style. Congratulations, you're in pretty good shape! Don't forget to look at your strong style, which is the next highest score. That's the one you'll need to examine.

If your style-seven diagram falls below one or more of the other six style scores, your work is cut out for you. But regardless of which styles are your predominant and strong styles, you can use the next part of this book as a practical resource to help yourself combat and overcome some of the ineffective ways you relate to your child.

Part Two—**HELP!**

10

Parent-Style Communication Patterns and What to Do About Them

Talk can cure, and talk can foster constructive change. But it must be the right kind of talk. How they (parents) talk to their children will determine whether they will be helpful or destructive.
The effective parent, like the effective counselor, must learn how to communicate his acceptance and acquire the same communication skills.

—Dr. Thomas Gordon

Communication Patterns—Laying the Groundwork

There are only two ways our children learn about the ways they're supposed to behave: they learn by actions and they learn by words. Unless you believe that children learn supernaturally or mystically, there aren't any other means we parents have at our disposal to teach children good behavior. Just as the different parent-styles show themselves in the actions of a parent, the parent-styles show up in the way parents communicate with children.

As social beings, the majority of our communication is verbal. We command, demand, boast, discuss, talk into, talk out of, talk for, talk against. We talk behind people's backs, out of both sides of our mouths, and, sometimes, off the tops of our heads. Regardless of how we talk, that act of verbal communication is the single most important way children learn, whether it be in school or at home. Since this book is for you—the parent—and not for teachers, I'd like to show you how each parent-style communicates with children, and why some parents have lost even before they open their mouths.

Instead of using the word *talking*, I call the child-parent communication process communication patterns, for two reasons: first, to avoid confusion with the characteristics of the talker-style parent, and, second, to emphasize that the whole process is far more than just talking.

Naturally, since I just gave my communication patterns its fancy name, I need some suitable lingo to go with it.

Statement: When a parent says something, or makes a remark, I call it a statement. For example, "Let's go to the movies" is a statement. And a statement is followed by a response, a result of the parent's statement.

Response: When the statement is, for example, "Let's go to the movies," the child's response might be "Yes, let's go, Mom!" or "When, tonight?" or any number of different responses.

With every statement and every response, there is an accompanying *underlying statement* (that goes with the statement) and an *underlying response* (that goes with the response). For example, the statement "Let's go to the movies" might have as its underlying statement ("Because I'm bored tonight"). And the underlying response made by the child would follow the child's response in the same way: "Yes, let's go, Mom!" ("I won't have to do my homework"). These terms indicate that when something is said aloud, there are feelings, undercurrents, and hidden thoughts that are unsaid. The underlying statement and the underlying response are unspoken statements and responses. From now on, I will enclose them in parentheses to set them off from the statements and responses.

Next is the *atmosphere*. When two people communicate—as parent and child are doing in the "Let's go to the movies" example—an atmosphere is created. In the movie example, it could be one of anticipation, excitement, or joy. Atmosphere describes feelings or sensations that are present as a result of the statement, underlying statement, response, and underlying response.

The *action* is the "what happens" as a result of all the above. In the same movie example, the action might be putting on coats and warming the car. In a violent communication, the action might be screaming.

Finally, we have the *outcome*, which signifies closure or completion of the discussion or communication. In the example of going to the movies, the outcome would be going to the movies. In a violent communication, the outcome might be spanking, running away, or murder.

The *final statement*, a part of the outcome, is the human feeling or understanding that exists as the result of the entire communication. Thus, the final statement in our movie example would be "That was fun. Let's do it again sometime!"

For the purpose of illustrating the communication patterns that occur within each parent-style, I will use the simple phrase "Let's talk" as the parent's statement for each of the parent-child communication patterns. By using the same "Let's talk" statement, we can get a clear idea of the different child responses and of the different atmospheres, actions, outcomes, and final statements for each of the style categories.

For the purposes of these illustrations, we will assume that the child and parent have been living together for a number of years and that the child and parent are of normal intelligence and sound mind. Last, we need to assume that the "Let's talk" statement comes as a result of the parent's desire to talk. No misbehavior is presumed to have happened.

Beginning with the style-seven parent communication pattern, we'll assume that the parent has initiated a conversation with "Let's talk."

The child's response is "Okay, let's talk." It's important to note that with the style-seven parent-child interchange, there is no underlying statement by the parent and no underlying response by the child. In contrast, if this were a martyr-style communication pattern, the child's underlying response might be ("What did I do now?"). Or, if this were a doctor-style communication pattern, the child's underlying response might be ("Uh-oh. Time to act grown-up.").

Just as the child has no underlying response in this communication pattern, the parent has no underlying statement. If the parent's statement is "Let's talk," then that's precisely what the parent wants to do, and both parent and child know that. The style-seven communication pattern needs no underlying statements or responses because the communication is right there— laid out on the table.

The atmosphere of the communication pattern between style-seven parent and child is one of mutual respect, caring, congeniality, sincerity, honesty, and mutual esteem. The child has no hidden, secret responses to make because he or she knows that the parent is not trying to pull anything. The parent is not trying to manipulate the child. The child does not feel threatened ("What did I do now?"), nor does the child sense that he or she must put on an act ("Uh-oh. Time to act grown-up.").

The action varies in this communication pattern; it depends on the subject at hand. There are no stereotyped actions with the style-seven communication pattern; in contrast, with the martyr-style pattern, the child or parent might pout, or put on a disgusted look, as if to say, "Here we go again." Did you ever see children roll their eyes in bored disgust whenever their parent said anything? That's the kind of unhealthy, stereotyped action seen in, for example, the martyr-style pattern.

The outcome of a style-seven communication pattern is not seen as a win-lose situation, as it is with other styles. The pattern is not conducted so that someone—parent or child—will be victorious; it's not a competition between parties, nor is it a situation designed to make one or both feel bad.

In contrast, with the doctor-style communication pattern, the outcome is polite—on the surface. A "reason" for the problem is established, and the problem is "solved." In the diplomat pattern, the child wins through appeasement, but the parent wins, too. In the autocrat pattern, the parent always wins; the child always loses. To repeat, the outcome of the style-seven pattern is one of satisfaction—for both parent and child.

There is no final statement in the style-seven communication pattern because nothing more needs to be said about the outcome. In the style-seven pattern, the outcome and the final statement are one and the same.

The final statement of the martyr-style communication pattern is "Are you satisfied with the unhappiness you've caused me?" when the parent wins. When the child is victorious, the final statement is "It's my fault—I'm such a bad parent."

Before we look at communication patterns for each style, let's look at the entire style-seven communication pattern.

STYLE-SEVEN STATEMENT:	"Let's talk." (No underlying statement.)
CHILD'S RESPONSE:	"Okay, let's talk." (No underlying response.)
ATMOSPHERE:	Mutual respect, caring, congeniality, sincerity, honesty, and esteem.
ACTION:	Depends on the matter at hand.
OUTCOME:	Understanding, cooperation, satisfaction, and usually agreement.
FINAL STATEMENT:	None needed. The outcome is the final statement.

Now that you can see the structure of the parent-child communication pattern, let's take another style-seven statement, said by a father to his teenage son: "I've made plans for my vacation time this July. We'll go to the mountains with the camper." As you read through the pattern, be aware of the lack of underlying statement and response and the positive atmosphere.

Style-Seven Communication Pattern

STYLE-SEVEN STATEMENT:	"I've made plans for my vacation time this July. We'll go to the mountains with the camper."
SON'S RESPONSE:	"I don't think I want to go, Dad. Is it really important that I go? If not, I'd rather stay with Steve and go swimming in his new pool."
ATMOSPHERE:	Honest expression of feelings.
ACTION:	Discussion. Parent: "You don't have to go with us. But how do Steve's parents feel about this?" Son: "I don't know. They've invited me before—I don't think they'll mind at all."
OUTCOME:	Resolution of difference. Parent: "Well, check with Mom. If it's okay with her, we can call Steve's parents." Son: "Thanks, Dad."

Admittedly, this is a simple example, but it shows at least three important aspects of the style-seven communication pattern.

Openness. Dad, in this example, was open to a change in his plan. He didn't rigidly hold to his idea. He wasn't trying to dominate the son, nor was the son interested in duping or deceiving Dad.

A Willingness to Take Risks. The parent in this example was not afraid to take a risk. He did not say, "Are you going to go on a drinking binge with Steve?" because he trusted his son. But Dad also knew that if his son were determined to drink, there would be little Dad could do about it. He didn't question his son's motives: "Why? Why do you want to go to Steve's?" He didn't take it personally when his son begged off the camping trip: "You mean you'd rather be with a friend instead of your family? Your own flesh and blood?" If Dad had felt that what his son wanted to do was dangerous, he would have spoken honestly about that concern to his son. If he had had doubts about his son's character, the pattern would have been different. Would there have been an argument? No, because his son would have known about those doubts before they started talking.

Flexibility. The outcome was that the son would check first with the other parent (Mom), and they would then check with Steve's parents. This outcome showed that the parent was in charge and that he was not being manipulated by his son. The son was not being coerced by Dad, and there was trust all around.

The next communication pattern between Dad and his son (if Steve's parents say yes, for example) will proceed well. Even if Steve's parents turn the boy down, no conflict will develop. The style-seven Dad will probably just ask his son what he wishes to do. And that's the way style-seven parents succeed. The son will never say, "You made me do this." Dad will never say, "That boy is driving me crazy!"

Taking our original "Let's talk" parent statement, we can see how it works with the child-style parent.

Child-Style Communication Pattern

CHILD-STYLE
PARENT STATEMENT: "Let's talk." ("Talk or I'll get mad at you.")

CHILD'S RESPONSE: "Okay." ("But I'd rather not because you're going to play parent with me again.")

ATMOSPHERE: Emotional, attempts at honesty or humor.

ACTION: Emotional responses—possibly tears—accusations, arguments.

OUTCOME: 1. A stalemate, or,
2. Parent loses, child wins.

FINAL STATEMENT: 1. None, or,
2. "Okay, this is your last chance, and I mean it!"

Most revealing is the parent's underlying statement, which, in effect, is saying "I'll get mad and tell on you if you don't cooperate!"—a kind of do-as-I-say-or-else threat that children engage in to control their friends or playmates.

Notice that the child's response is different from the child's underlying response. Although the child says "Okay," he or she knows very well the way in which his or her parent operates. The child's underlying response doesn't mean that he or she is bad or snotty or fresh. It's a natural reaction that has developed from the interaction between the child and the child-style parent over a period of time. Unless the parent changes the style, the child's stereotyped underlying response will continue.

Even the atmosphere resembles one in which two children are talking—emotional at times, with attempts at honesty or humor. If the parent's statement were an accusation, like "You didn't make your bed!" instead of "Let's talk," the atmosphere might include crying or tension.

As might be expected, the action can grow into an argument, depending on the subject. The child-style parent has not built up a reservoir of respect, and the child knows it. The parent is not seen as a legitimate authority figure—someone worthy of the power that comes with parenthood. Instead, the child-style parent is seen as a comrade, and when that comrade attempts to act like an authoritative parent, the child's response is "Who do you think you are? The boss?"

The outcome is often a stalemate; sometimes, though, through sheer perseverance, the child wins. When a stalemate occurs, there's no final statement (just bad feelings); but when the child wins, the parent says something like "Okay, this is your last chance. Don't ask me to do this [or let you do this] again." When, as part of the final statement, the parent says "and I mean it!" the child knows that that just isn't so, and he or she will prove it with the next communication pattern. Unless the child-style parent breaks out of this rut, the same type of ineffective communication patterns will recur.

Doctor-Style Communication Pattern

DOCTOR-STYLE PARENT STATEMENT:	"Let's talk." ("Let's be adult about this matter.")
CHILD'S RESPONSE:	"Okay, let's talk." ("Uh-oh. Time to act grown-up.")
ATMOSPHERE:	Rational, often clinical, diagnostic, unemotional.
ACTION:	Causes and reasons sought—through discussion—for the problem at hand.
OUTCOME:	Polite closure: A diagnosis is established, the problem "solved." Child sometimes wins when talking it over replaces punishment for misbehavior.
FINAL STATEMENT:	"I hope this has taught you a valuable lesson, Son."

Diplomat-Style Communication Pattern

DIPLOMAT-STYLE PARENT STATEMENT:	"Let's talk." ("What's he got up his sleeve this time?")
CHILD'S RESPONSE:	"Okay, let's talk." ("What's he got up his sleeve this time?")
ATMOSPHERE:	Distrust, calm but suspicious, careful.
ACTION:	Answers are sought through discussion. Parent attempts manipulation; child is usually successful at manipulating parent.
OUTCOME:	Parent gives in if child insists.
FINAL STATEMENT:	"All right, I'll do it this time, but don't ask me again."

Autocrat-Style Communication Pattern

AUTOCRAT-STYLE PARENT STATEMENT:	"Let's talk." ("There's really nothing to talk about. I'm boss, and my child better not defy me.")
CHILD'S RESPONSE:	"Okay, let's talk." ("There's nothing to talk about . . . you always win; someday, I'm gonna win. . . .")
ATMOSPHERE:	Stiff, strict, tense, adversary.
ACTION:	One-sided lecturing, reprimanding, commanding, parental domination.
OUTCOME:	Parent wins, child loses.
FINAL STATEMENT:	"Don't let this happen again. You'll get it worse next time!"

Martyr-Style Communication Pattern

MARTYR-STYLE PARENT STATEMENT:	"Let's talk." ("Why is this happening to me? Why me?")
CHILD'S RESPONSE:	"Do we have to?" ("What did I do now?")
ATMOSPHERE:	Emotional, tense, guilt-laden, self-righteous action.
ACTION:	Blame is projected and/or accepted.
OUTCOME:	1. Parent wins, child loses (dominant martyr-style). Parent wins by making child feel guilty for causing parent's grief. 2. Child wins, parent loses (submissive martyr-style). Child wins by successfully allowing parent to accept blame.
FINAL STATEMENT:	1. "Are you satisfied with the unhappiness you've caused me?" 2. "It's my fault—I'm such a bad parent."

Talker-Style Communication Pattern

TALKER-STYLE PARENT STATEMENT:	"Let's talk."
CHILD'S RESPONSE:	"Let's not." ("I'm sick of hearing your voice. I wish you would shut your trap

for a while. I don't want to hear you rant and rave . . .")

ATMOSPHERE: Avoidance, tuning out, guilt.

ACTION: Parent talks, child doesn't listen. Or, both talk, neither listens.

OUTCOME: Parent loses, child wins. Or, both lose.

FINAL STATEMENT: Parent: "Go ahead and do it. Don't say I didn't warn you." Child: "Just get off my back . . ."

How to Change Ineffective Communication Patterns

To change an ineffective parent-style, start with your communication pattern. Look at the way you talk to and with your child. Use the unsuccessful communication patterns I've just presented as guides. You won't find yourself described perfectly by any of them, but you can use the patterns to identify what goes on in your own life with your child. How is the way your child relates to you similar to the sample communication patterns? How is the way you relate to your child similar to those patterns? Although there are no hard-and-fast rules, I have some practical suggestions to help you look at, and modify, your ineffective communication patterns.

Ask yourself, How closely do those sample communication patterns resemble my communication with my child? Which pattern(s) seems to be closest to the way I talk with my child? In short, identify the pattern(s) that comes closest to your communication style.

Now, identify the defective component. What part of the pattern seems to be the problem area? Most parents blunder with the first component—the statement—and it's all downhill from there.

STATEMENTS: BLUNDERS AND REMEDIES

Here are some examples of statement blunders.

"So, you're going out again."
"I heard all about your behavior in school today."
"Going to see your hoodlum boyfriend?"
"Please don't get drunk tonight."
"Still seeing that tramp?"

Statements are indicators as to the way that the pattern will go. The majority of unsatisfactory communication patterns can be avoided by using proper statements. If you hope to change anything in the way you and your child communicate, you must first change your challenging, sarcastic, insincere, or inappropriate statements. Here's how.

Think of the one-liners you've shot at your child and ask yourself, What self-respecting human being would not be insulted by my snotty remarks? Just for a moment, put yourself in your child's place and hear how your statements sound. If they're unkind, change them. Instead of saying "I heard all about your behavior in school today," which can be taken many different ways, be more specific, honest, and noninsulting: "John, I'm really concerned about the way you've been behaving in school."

If your child is used to your sarcasm or insincere statements, surprise him or her. Instead of saying "Are you in trouble again?" say "You look as if you've had a rough day. Want to talk about it?" If your child has grown accustomed to your style, a change will throw him or her for a loop. Although the child's response may not show it, odds are that he or she will be puzzled by your statement change. Be persistent; be patient. Your new statements will yield results in a very short time.

Think before you speak. Get in the habit of saying your intended statement to yourself before blurting it out. Don't be blunt—be honest.

Address your child by his or her first name. Some children get used to being spoken to without a first name. "Hey, you" does nicely for some parents. Avoid it. Use your child's name. If you've been calling him or her by a nickname since birth, does he or she like it? If not, eliminate it. When you issue forth one of your new statements, start it with your child's first name.

Avoid sarcasm. It's amazing how many adults think that sarcasm and humor are the same. Even if you mean your sarcasm lightly, avoid it. Sarcasm could very well set off child responses that you never wanted. And then comes the real argument. For example:

> PARENT STATEMENT: (Lightly—looking at another bad report card) I see you got another good report card.
>
> CHILD'S RESPONSE: (Sullen) It's not good—it's bad.
>
> CHILD'S UNDERLYING RESPONSE: (Why don't you shut up? You're just as bad as my dumb teacher.)

Watch your statements. They set the tone for the whole communication pattern.

RESPONSES: BLUNDERS AND REMEDIES

Response blunders are defective answers to parent statements. Whether spoken or unspoken, they serve to malign the communication pattern. The child can respond to your statement with silence, as when the child is trying to ignore something you're saying; or his or her response can be combined with an underlying response, as with the child who both thinks and says "Leave me alone."

A response blunder is the child's blunder. As such, you cannot directly control it; you can't put words in the child's mouth. (But some autocrat-style parents try.)

Although you cannot directly control response blunders, you can control your own statement blunders. Therefore, to avoid many children's response blunders, you must make sincere, honest, and nonsarcastic statements.

If you find that after changing your statements, your child still comes back with disrespectful responses, stop him or her with "That's not the kind of talk that I will allow" or "I spoke with respect to you. I expect the same."

Your child will eventually get the message that your way of talking to him or her has changed. Patience and firmness are important at this time. Don't continue the conversation if you get a negative, disrespectful, or sarcastic response. Stop the conversation, point out why the answer you got is unacceptable, and don't harp on it! Within a short time, your child will learn how to make productive responses.

UNDERLYING STATEMENTS AND RESPONSES: BLUNDERS AND REMEDIES

Since these two components of the communication pattern involve feelings more than words, there's not much you can do to influence them directly. They will change as your statements and your child's responses change. If you've changed your statements, you have taken the biggest, most important step toward modifying the underlying statements and responses.

ATMOSPHERE: BLUNDERS AND REMEDIES

What's an atmospheric blunder? Body language, like folding your arms across the chest, or trying to talk when the baby is screaming, when your spouse is upset, when the television is blaring, or when the cat is using the potted palm for a litter box.

The atmosphere is influenced by the statements and responses—underlying and otherwise. Usually, the more sensitive and caring your statements, the better the atmosphere.

But some parents compound their statement blunders by adding atmospheric blunders. It's hard enough to be concerned about being an effective parent and about communicating well with your child without having to worry about atmospheric blunders. Nobody needs them, especially parents trying to improve their communication pattern.

Here are some guidelines for avoiding atmospheric blunders.

Talk when you're calm—not when you're angry or when you're thinking about how to make next month's mortgage or rent payment. I've seen it time and time again in school. A nervous teacher seems to have a jumpy class. A slow-moving and deliberate teacher has a class with a calm demeanor. It's hard enough to communicate—don't add more outside static from the atmosphere.

What does your face look like when you are with your child? This sounds physically impossible, but watch your face. Look at a mirror and say, "John, take out the garbage." Look at a mirror and say, "Shirl, please pick up your underwear." Say it the way you always say it. What do you look like? Are you adding to the atmosphere in a positive way? Or are you setting the stage for a Greek tragedy?

Is your voice loud? Is it too soft and meek? Is your tone accusing? Your voice is a key part of the atmosphere. Listen to yourself talk. You don't need a professional voice instructor. Just as you looked at your face in the mirror, look at your voice by using a tape recorder. Yes, that's what you sound like. Don't blame it on tape distortion. Practice talking softly; practice changing from a stern voice to a kind voice.

Even if you're not a talker-style parent, consider the fact that you might talk too much when you talk to your children. Keep what you've got to say short and sweet and to the point. Even doctor-style, diplomat-style, and martyr-style parents sometimes talk too much.

If, for example, your husband is under the sink struggling and groaning as he tries to loosen a pipe, you wouldn't bend over him and say, "Five checks have bounced." Or, if your wife has just burned her leg as a cup of hot tea tipped over, you wouldn't say, "Please pick up the baby—he's crying." Thus, when Joey comes home with a poor report card, or when his best friend has just gone off without him, don't—right then—sternly remind him of his responsibility to clean up his room. Postpone the discussion until the atmosphere improves.

ACTIONS AND OUTCOMES: BLUNDERS AND REMEDIES

The action is what happens in a discussion as a result of the statements and the atmosphere. The different action blunders will generally depend on your parent-style, your statement, and your child's response. If your communication pattern got off to a good start, chances are both the action and the outcome will be satisfactory.

Hitting is one action you'll need to watch. Sometimes you're upset—no doubt about it. And you're angry. And you don't want to wait for the right atmosphere. Remember, though, that if you resort to hitting as an action or an outcome, you'll be teaching your child that hitting solves problems, that it's okay to hit when you're angry. You'll also be making it more and more difficult for your child ever to listen to what you say. If he or she takes you seriously only when you strike out and hit, you're setting yourself up for a lifetime of having to hit. Children learn from our behavior, and they can learn aggressive behavior (like hitting) from us. Dr. Albert Bandura, professor of psychology at Stanford University, said, "People do not come equipped with inborn aggressive skills. They must learn them. Most behavior is learned observationally through the power of example. This is particularly true of aggression. . . ."

If you're so angry you want to strike your child, give yourself a time-out. Do something—right away. Leave the room, wax the piano, empty the litter box, or scream out the window. Don't hit. It's never worth it.

Spanking? It's the only exception to the rule. Sure, spanking is a form of hitting, but it's purposeful (to secure discipline but never for retaliation), and it's directed at the child's buttocks. Depending on the child's age, the "crime," and the circumstances, most experts feel that only in rare moments is it a good idea. It has a legitimate place in child rearing, but not when it's overused or abusive. Most important, remind yourself of the difference between hitting and spanking.

If, after you've taken the steps outlined above to help make successful communication patterns, you find that you're still not happy with the outcome or action, go back to your statements. If you are still not satisfied with your action and outcome, go back to your child's response. Don't tolerate rude or sarcastic responses after you've changed your statements. But don't try to change your child's responses or underlying responses if you haven't changed your statements. It won't work.

Conclusion

There is no one perfect way to communicate. Obviously, what happens when parent and child talk depends to a great extent on the particular parent and child involved in the communication. But, when child and parent are used to communicating with each other over a period of years, stereotyped patterns develop. The child adapts to the parent-style with which he or she has had to deal for all his or her life.

For example, a student behaves very differently with a new teacher in September compared with the way he or she behaves with that same teacher in June. What's the difference? The child has gotten used to the teacher's behavior, used to his or her teacher-style. Communication patterns occur over and over again from September on; by January, the child-teacher pattern is relatively set. I have seen teachers shake their heads in June and say, "Nothing I did or said had an effect on that child." Parents, however, don't have the luxury of being able to promote their children or transfer them to other teachers.

11
Practical Help
for Your
Parent-Style

Children need models rather than critics.

—Joseph Joubert

On the following pages are statements by parents and questions that they frequently ask me, grouped according to each parent-style. Since most of the questions I receive are in question form, I have reproduced the questions almost exactly as they were asked. Each set is presented in the same order as the parent-styles have been presented: child, doctor, diplomat, autocrat, martyr, and talker.

Statements were selected based on two factors—first, on the frequency with which they have come up in my dealings with parents and children, and, second, on their ability to provide practical help for the reader. I know you'll profit from some of the suggestions, strategies, and tactics I've outlined ahead.

Child-Style Statements

"My children are constantly accusing me of not being fair. No matter how hard I try, nothing seems to help."

Telling you that you're not being fair is a device used by your children to control your behavior. Your children continue to make this accusation for one very important reason: It works. It makes you work harder for them; it pushes your buttons. You give in to their demands despite their continued accusations. Why? Because you love your children and want to show it. Dr. Fitzhugh Dodson, author of *How to Discipline—with Love,* explains the technique this way: "The type of parent who is constantly appeasing a child, giving in to the child's whims and demands, and letting the child push her around is doing this for a basic psychological reason. Deep down she is operating on this unconscious motto: *If I don't do what my child wants, he won't love me.*" There is no better practical advice I can give than this: Simply stop giving in to that line. When a child accuses you of not being fair, don't argue. Don't try to convince him or her, either by your words or by your actions, that you are trying to be fair.

Consider the following example. During a cold spell, the second-grade class went outside for morning recess. Later in the day, the temperature dropped several more degrees, and the wind was howling. When it was time for the other classes to go out for recess, I told the teachers to have their classes stay inside. A student from one of those classes met me in the hall and said, "Mr. DiGiulio, you're not being fair. You let Miss Black's class go out, but you're not letting us go out for recess." I told her, "Sally, the temperature is very low, and it's dropping. Maybe tomorrow will be sunny and warmer." With that, Sally said, "I sure hope so—we've got to finish our soccer game!" With a smile, she turned and went on her way.

If I had said, "I am too being fair," I would just have gotten into a no-win argument. If I had said, "How *dare* you question me?" I would have hurt her feelings. Brief, truthful answers—not long explanations or defensive comebacks—work best. And they work for parents, too.

> "But, what if the child doesn't approve? I mean, what if Sally still thought you were being unfair?"

If Sally felt that I was unfair, I would not try to convince her that I *was* being fair. There's no way that I could do so, even if I tried. That would be her problem, not mine. If she still was not satisfied by my explanation, I would conclude that she was out to prove a point or to get me into a conflict. If she still persisted, I'd simply say again, "Sally, it's too cold outside." I would not offer excuses; I would not promise her that tomorrow would be a fair day; I would not change my mind—not because I'm stubborn, but because I am the responsible adult in this instance. Another possibility would be for me to walk Sally back to her teacher to find out "what exciting activities Mrs. Appleby has planned for this stay-in recess." Without compromising myself, I would direct Sally's attention to the positive side of staying in.

> "My son's behavior is horrible. I hate to punish him, and when he says he's sorry and asks for one more chance, I give in. But he just never seems to learn."

Many child-style parents abhor punishments. Punishing their children makes them feel like bullies; they worry that they're being too strict with their children. But setting limits and enforcing them is one of the most crucial things a parent needs to learn when dealing with children—especially difficult children. Limits should be specific and to the point, for example, "You are not to leave the house until I come back home." Limits must be appropriate. "You are not to go into the street" is appropriate for a four-year-old; it is not appropriate for a fifteen-year-old. Conversely, "You are to be home by eleven" is appropriate for a teenager, and it's specific as well. Limits need to be enforceable. "Don't stay at Johnny's house too long" is not a limit because it's debatable as to how long "too long" really is. A better limit would be "Please be home by five." Last, and most important, limits must be enforced. That's the crux of this whole process. This does not necessarily mean that you must punish—that depends on the nature of the limit. The late Dr. Haim Ginott, author of the landmark work *Between Parent and Child,* speaks of limits: "A limit must be stated firmly, so that it carries only one message to the child: 'This prohibition is for real. I mean business.'" He continues: "A limit must be stated in a manner that is deliberately calculated to minimize resentment and to save self-esteem. The very process of limit setting should convey authority, not insult. It should deal with a specific event." Giving a child just one more chance can never be justified, because if you set your limit correctly the first time, there's no need for another chance. If the child exceeds the limit (or breaks the rule), he or she must face the consequences. If you give in, you're not being a pushover—you're being dishonest.

> "But when I *do* tell him that he has broken my rules, the only one who can control him is my husband. I don't think he thinks I'm serious."

You're absolutely right. If your husband is the only one who can control him, your child isn't taking you seriously. Here's what to do: nothing—at least for a while. Stop where you are and make no more rules or limits for a day or so. If your child is not going to listen, there's no point in going on the same way. Plan your strategy, because when you set the next limit, you're going to enforce it. Pick something that you know you can and will enforce. "Your room must be cleaned before you go outside. I'm serious. You may not go outside unless it's clean—clothes put away and bed made." Focus on one statement like the one I've just mentioned. Check the child's room before you allow him to go out. If it's not cleaned, don't let him off the hook. Sure, he'll complain and maybe cry or even scream. But if you enforce the limit this time, I guarantee that he'll scream a little less and shed fewer tears next time when he tries to walk out with his room dirty. It takes time and patience.

Just keep reminding yourself that if you rely on another person (like Daddy), you're sunk. You will lose your ability to have any effect on your child's behavior. In an article, "A Chance to Be Good," in *The Single Parent* magazine, I advised parents: "When firm discipline is needed, rely on yourself and nobody else! Refrain from delegating your authority and responsibility as a parent to anyone else—your child's teacher, principal, scoutmaster, or any other adult."

For example, as the principal of an elementary school, I have been asked more than a few times to become involved in issues that should have been settled at home. Parents have asked me to punish children for offenses committed outside of school, and some have asked me to "keep Johnny in at recess" because of some misbehavior at home. I would never agree with such a request. (On the other hand, when a child misbehaves at school, don't let the school tell you what to do at home for punishment. I would never ask a parent to punish a child at home for breaking a school rule.)

> "Mr. DiGiulio, I love Mary and she knows it. Ever since she was born, I have made sure I hugged her at least once a day. When she was a baby and a toddler, she was a joy. But now, no matter how much love, affection, and security I try to give her, she behaves horribly at times—answering back and defying my authority."

Many, many child-style parents are loving, warm parents. No question about it. Unfortunately, though, they tend to place emphasis on love's ability to control behavior. Actually, love has no ability to do that, nor should love be used as a reason why someone should behave or follow a set of rules. "To love and obey" is part of the traditional wedding vow; maybe the child-style parent has taken "love and obey" as a guiding light for all members of the family.

Parents who feel cheated, having given so much of their time and love, often feel that there should be some compensation for all that loving.

Ellen Peck, the author of several books in the family-planning field, and Dr. William Granzig, associate director of medical education for the American College of Obstetricians and Gynecologists, have done some interesting investigations into parents who look for "magic moments" in parenting: "Successful parents said that such times [magic moments] are not what parenthood is all about. They viewed child rearing as an over-all process. They did not expect a few landmark occasions to compensate for continuing challenges and difficulties. One mother criticized 'the photograph-album approach' to parenthood, in which only the special events are recorded at all, and only the best versions of these are preserved."

Child-style parents are often guilty of this photograph-album approach because they tend to dwell on the positive, happy, hugging things in their child's life—not facing the boring home routines or the difficult challenges that even a "hugged" child presents.

I'd advise the parent in this example to institute an I-love-you-but-here's-the-limit policy. My suspicion is that Mary is controlling Mother, and not vice versa. I'd advise this parent to follow the same course of action as the parent in the second example who had difficulty setting and enforcing limits. The title of Bruno Bettelheim's book says it all: *Love Is Not Enough.*

> "I don't know what to tell my son about sex. He's definitely old enough, and I want him to learn it in a wholesome way. I've always had a pretty honest relationship with him, and I don't want to mislead him. Frankly, the subject scares me."

There's no doubt that sex is a delicate subject for many parents. But there's even less doubt that sex education should be taught by parents, because schools—despite the trend toward sex education—can't do the job nearly so well as parents can. Parents know their children's limits of understanding better than anyone else, including teachers.

I recommend giving as much information as you can comfortably give. Arm yourself with a book. Read it before you talk with your child. There's one book on the subject that I think is especially good: *When Children Ask About Sex—A Guide for Parents*, by Joae Graham Selzer, M.D. It gives information that's suitable for preschoolers to preteens and even gets into sex and limits for teens. But, book or no book, don't ignore your child's questions. "Go ask Daddy [or Mommy]" is not a suitable answer. Perhaps you will want to decide which parent feels more comfortable with the subject. But don't surprise your spouse by channeling your child's questions to him or her.

> "Sometimes I feel like giving up. There are times when I feel like I have no control over my two sons, no control over my life at all. If I had to do it over again, I would not let everyone, mostly my kids, be in charge. I feel like a victim."

This parent says something that many child-style parents feel at one time or another. But he or she is wrong on one count: it's not too late to turn things around, no matter how old the sons are. In fact, if they're teenagers, they might better understand this parent's new stance. In order to get to that point, this child-style parent needs very much to say, "From now on, I count, too." If you're in the same position as this child-style parent, the following exercises and suggestions may help you get out of your rut. For starters, list at least five things you do, not because you want to, but because of other people—for example, baby-sitting for a neighbor's child in emergencies that are not really emergencies, bringing your son's lunch or homework to school at ten o'clock when he forgets, or driving your daughter to school when she misses the school bus. Now write down some ways you could avoid doing those things—saying "No, I'm sorry. I'm busy tonight" to your emergency-prone neighbor, letting your son go without lunch, and letting your daughter know she must face the consequences (depending on her age) for missing school.

The child-style parent is particularly prone to being a doormat, due to his or her kind, warm, loving, and childlike perspective. But, the child-style parent can take charge of his or her life without losing any honesty, love, or warmth.

Take your list and the alternatives, and, starting with your children (don't start with a husband or wife—children are far more flexible), decide on a date and time to begin change number one. Pick only one item at a time. Clearly tell your child what the change will involve. Say, for example, "I will no longer pick up your underwear." Tell your child—shortly and sweetly—what this change will mean to him or her. "You will put your own underwear into the hamper." Inform him or her what the consequences will be if he or she doesn't cooperate. "I will wash all clothes that are in the hamper. If your underwear is not there, it will not be washed." As I said before, limits must be enforced. If you go back on your word just once, your rules are useless; you will be bending for underwear for the rest of your natural days.

Through personal experience, I learned that this method works. My mother did it to me. I washed my own underwear in a hurry one morning (I didn't think she was serious; she was), and I dried it in the oven. All day long I smelled like burned toast.

Doctor-Style Statements

"I work all day, and my son absolutely refuses to do any helping around the house. Not even the dishes! When I ask why, he just says it's 'woman's work'. He always has an answer for me—I get nowhere."

This parent came into my office recently and told me all the "why" questions she asked her son each day. I was amazed that the child still responded to her at all. An integral part of the doctor-style parent's defective style, the need to ask why is a sure dead end because it paves the way for making excuses—

and more excuses. Consequently, the misbehavior is never discussed or confronted. In this example, the son's refusal on the grounds that it's "woman's work" is baloney. He's copping out, and he knows it.

Following is an example from school. You see, teachers are often the worst sinners in this why business. (I was tempted to call this style the teacher-style parent instead of the doctor-style.) Here is a dialogue that might give you some insight into that useless word.

> TEACHER: Jason, why are you turning around?
>
> JASON: Ian took my pencil.
>
> TEACHER: Ian, why did you take Jason's pencil?
>
> IAN: Because Jason took mine!
>
> JASON (ANGRY): I did not, you liar!
>
> TEACHER: Hold it. Jason, why are you calling names?
>
> JASON (ANGRIER): Because . . .

The teacher in this case got herself into a bind, interrupted her lesson, got two children angry at her and at each other, and now she's got a potential fight on her hands—all because of that stupid word.

Whether you're a teacher or a parent, deal with the misbehavior and not the reasons for it. First, the child just may not know why he or she did something, or, the child may not want to admit that he or she misbehaved because he or she was bored or was being a prankster. Second, because knowing the reason doesn't really help you get to the bottom of things, trying to determine the cause of behavior is a waste of energy. The teacher should have dealt with the misbehavior (Jason's not paying attention) and not with the whys. Similarly, the mother whose son will not wash dishes is just giving him a perfect out by allowing him to tell her why. As with the child-style parent, this parent needs to get tough, to set limits ("I will no longer wash dishes every night; you will have to take your share") and enforce them. She should give the boy a choice. Let him drink his coffee from dirty cups, use his hands, or wash the dishes—and she shouldn't let him off the hook.

> "Mr. DiGiulio, I want Karl to have everything I never had. I had a bad childhood, and my family didn't have two nickels to their name. I want to be the best possible parent—he deserves a perfect parent."

Called in to speak with me about Karl's misbehavior, which was not serious, his mother, Mrs. Thomas, thought it was a reflection on her "perfection" as a parent. I knew Mrs. Thomas, a single parent, was not well off financially, yet Karl's clothes were expensive; I'd noticed he had very expensive skiwear and ski equipment. She was moonlighting to keep Karl in those neat duds, and she was upset about her inability to spend more time with Karl, her occasional arguments at home with him, and, in general, her "failings," as she saw them. Mrs. Thomas wanted to be the ideal parent.

I say that it's a totally losing proposition to want to be ideal or perfect. I assured Mrs. Thomas that Karl's school problems were not severe, and even if they had been, they were Karl's problems, not hers. After a long talk, Mrs. Thomas seemed to have a better perspective on the value of Karl's being at the top of the heap in terms of material goods. She admitted that her second job was probably unnecessary and that she was thinking of quitting.

Two weeks later, she called to tell me that she'd quit her second job and was able—for the first time in four years—to be home with her son by five o'clock.

If you're a doctor-style parent who's striving to be ideal, make similar changes in your life—even if they mean you'll have less money. Look at what's really important. In Karl's case, what good were material things if friction between mother and son was reaching a tense point?

"Gene is a bright boy; I know he's doing well in school, but at times I worry—he seems so immature for his age."

Parents often worry about whether or not their children are mature, are at grade level, play with kids their age, and so on. Actually, there's no problem if a child prefers to be with younger children, or if he or she would rather watch "Sesame Street" than "Sixty Minutes."

Is Gene immature? It depends. It depends on what behavior or behaviors Father notices and his son's age. Gene's father was concerned about Gene's bed-wetting. Since Gene is twelve years old, I suggested it was not unusual for it to happen, but that it wasn't a minor concern either, given Gene's difficulty in getting along with kids his own age and other minor behavior problems the teacher and I had noticed. I suggested that Gene's father speak with a professional—starting with his family physician—to get a handle on Gene's situation.

Speaking of the sticky problem of "Where do I seek professional help?"—I think the best place to start is with your family physician. Teachers and principals see a lot of behavior and can be very helpful. But school personnel don't see the physiological side of the child. I have worked closely with physicians who have been superb in their cooperation and in their interest in children.

However, parents of children who have had a clean bill of health from physicians have come to me, apprehensive about some behavior not noticed by anyone but the parents. Where do you draw the line? If you feel that some behavior is abnormal (and I'm including the too good or too well-behaved, too quiet little girl who sits like a stone in school), and you can't quite put your finger on it, seek a second opinion from your husband, your wife, your child's teacher, a minister or priest, or the school counselor. If after getting this second opinion, you have the slightest doubt, take action. You can consult an agency (such as the Children's Aid Society, which provides individual and family counseling) before involving your child. Don't consult a psychologist at the drop of a hat, but, on the other hand, don't wait if you feel you have a legitimate question about your child.

> "My home is really neat, Mr. D. You should see my new swimming pool. I get whatever I want, but I'm not spoiled! Well, the only thing is sometimes my family doesn't seem real. I know my parents love me because they tell me they do, but I wonder sometimes."

I have seen a number of children (like Kevin) from "neat" homes. The parents are often college-educated professionals; both have well-paying careers; they have regular rap sessions with their kids. Frequently, though, the children of parents like these are unsure of themselves, unsure of their parents' love. Mom and Dad never fight, nor are there any arguments. This is the problem of the too-perfect home. I'm not saying that doctor-style parents should look for problems, but if you feel that something in your child's emotional development is lacking, look into it. The odds are that you're probably doing many things correctly, but, for a variety of reasons, your child might feel out of touch with you. Your parent-style is probably not the central point here; rather, it might be your family processes. You might benefit from seeing a professional family or individual therapist, counselor, or psychologist.

Instead of talking over this situation with Kevin (as I was sure Mom and Dad had done), I called his parents. Dad said, "Yes, we have been discussing this." I told him that I thought he might want to talk with a family therapist.

If you feel that something is really wrong, or even if it's something you can't quite put your finger on, the best advice I can give you is to check with a professional.

> "Why is Michelle a year behind in reading? What is the problem? Is it her teacher? The school? Maybe it's something I'm doing wrong with her?"

This was a real toughie. This doctor-style parent was willing to do anything possible for Michelle. Mother was willing to get help—tutors, psychologists, or private school—for her daughter. What did Mother want of me? She just wanted me to tell her what the problem was.

Mother wanted a simple, black-and-white solution for her child's deficiency in reading level. We had gone over all the teacher's reports, Michelle's past report cards, and all her test scores. We spent almost a half hour discussing Michelle's aptitude, which was only slightly below average. Mother's expectations, however, were way above that. Despite the fact that we discussed the many factors that go into the learning of reading (readiness, actual ability level, home, interests, heredity, teacher competency, and so on), Mother still wanted to zero in on the single problem behind Michelle's reading deficiency. I had no simple answer because there was none.

The problem may have been more with Mother than with Michelle. I saw no signs of a disturbed personality in Michelle; she was in perfect health and was sociable, friendly, and all the rest. Aside from the fact that she wasn't an exceptional reader, I saw little wrong with Michelle.

This kind of situation crops up with other kinds of behavior, and I believe that doctor-style parents are missing the point if they concentrate on a single problem as a cause for misbehaving. A teenager who smokes cigarettes behind his or her parents' backs is not smoking just because he or she "hangs around with Benny." Getting rid of Benny will not stop your child from smoking. Benny is not the problem.

A child's fighting over toys is not necessarily the result of the sound spanking the child got yesterday. The spanking was not *the reason.*

If anything, when we look for the one and only reason or try to find out what the problem is, we're going to miss it entirely. Just like Michelle's "reading problem"—it wasn't so much that Michelle couldn't read as it was the fact that Mother could not understand, or accept the fact, that other children scored higher than Michelle.

Diplomat-Style Statements

"My Dad and I get along; we talk a lot. But it seems that sometimes he's not really listening to me—he's thinking about something to convince me that everything is all right. I wish he was honest with me. Most of the time, I really don't know how he feels about things."

The famous family therapist Virginia Satir spoke to this child's concern. In her book *Peoplemaking,* Satir pointed out four key factors in all of the troubled families she'd seen. One of those key factors was that "communication was indirect, vague, and not really honest."

Although this lack of directness and honesty is not a behavior problem as such, it can lead to a child's resorting to the same technique he or she sees in the parents. For example, the child may lie, especially if he or she sees his or her parents engaged in bending the truth or telling little white lies.

Examine your style of talking. Are you sometimes evasive? Do you often renege on your word? Get rid of as many "maybe," "sometimes," "we'll see," and "I'm not promising" statements as you can. Start small. Make a commitment that you won't break. Many times we use indirect words (like *maybe)* when we're afraid to say no, but a truthful, honest no is better than ten *maybes.*

"I have been using behavior modification techniques since I took a course in parenting. When my son behaved well, I gave him a reward. It worked for a while, but he now expects something almost every day—just about every time he does a job at home."

It sounds as if what started out as behavior modification has been turned into a bribery situation. This may have happened because the rewards were given too frequently, so that the son has come to expect each positive behavior to be rewarded. One of the dangers of using behavior modification is that sometimes the subject of the experiment controls the experimenter. The underlying message is "If you don't give me my reward for being good, I'll be bad." That's the reason why—unless you've really got the system down pat and know what you're doing—I don't recommend behavior modification. It's too difficult to control.

If the situation gets out of hand, as it has in this example, drop the technique that's causing problems and substitute another. Give praise in place of those rewards. Use a big hug for a job well done. But don't give in if your child demands a reward.

"It's very hard for me to say no and mean it. When my child really wants something, and I say no, all he has to do is say 'But Mommy I love you'—or something like that— and I turn to jelly. I don't mind showing love this way, but I hate myself for it later on."

First of all, Mother is not showing her love by giving in. She wants peace, at any price, and sooner or later she will have to pay for it. As the years go by, the price of peace will keep increasing, and it will be more difficult to attain. What is the most essential step this parent can take?

I would advise this parent, and others with the same problem, to say no and mean it—to say no and not go back on it—to say no and not feel like a dictator —to say no and not feel guilty about it. When the child asks for something or is about to do something that you don't approve of, stop and think before you speak up. This way, your no will be honest—it will not be something you've said impulsively that you'll regret or have to go back on later. As I mentioned before, saying no is setting a limit for the child, and when the no is enforced, that limit is enforced as well.

From my article "A Chance to Be Good": " 'No' means 'No.' Not 'maybe'; not 'never'; not 'yes.' Saying *no* and meaning it is sometimes difficult but is one of the most important techniques to be learned in dealing with children. A child who throws a tantrum in a supermarket because his parent said 'No' probably has good reason to believe that the 'No' *really* means: 'You'll get your way if you are insistent. If you keep screaming, you're bound to get a *yes*.' How often have you seen such a scene?"

When Mother tells Junior no (in our original statement), and he says something like "I love you," Mother should turn to him and say, sincerely, "And I love you, too," meanwhile making no move toward buying Junior the item he wants. Junior's likely response will be a more emphatic "But I love you, Mommy." Mother should get ready because the first time this new technique is used, and Junior doesn't get his way, there'll probably be a tidal wave of emotion from Junior. He may be confused and frustrated; he may cry, throw a tantrum, or refuse to continue walking. Mother should say nothing and guide Junior out of the store. I recommend practicing this first at home, since there's a danger of Mother's giving in if this happens in a store with everyone watching. Start saying no at home.

Just remember, it gets better. The next time there will be less fuss and, depending on Junior's ability to hang on to a good thing, he will eventually accept it as part of his life with Mother. (This works for fathers, too, though we've used Mother as an example.)

This technique works, but it requires that you be patient and persistent. It's the only way to break this form of child domination. The earlier you do it in your child's life, the better.

> "I can't get my daughter to do her homework. Actually, the problem is not with her so much as it's with my feelings toward the homework she gets. I can't see the use in her doing long reports for French class when she wants to be a pianist. I'm torn because I know homework is important for an eighth-grade child. But I know she'd rather play her records than do homework. What's really more important—her music or her homework?"

This parent's dilemma touches on two areas—homework (the now) and music (the now and the future). First, homework. I know that homework is a controversial issue. Some parents feel it is important; other parents feel that a child's workday should end in school. Some parents feel that homework is an intrusion into the family's life, and I know what they mean. Practically speaking, though, the assignment has been given, and it should be completed. It's viewed as a legitimate part of the child's schoolwork and theoretically has educational value or it would not have been assigned. The value of French to, say, a potential pianist can be compared with the value of any academic subject—English, social studies, mathematics, and so on. We need to keep in mind that our children will need to interact with the society around them and that being fully educated will be a big plus, regardless of whether they become pianists, physicians, or fire fighters. I would advise this parent to make sure that the child has enough time to listen to music and play the piano. Is it possible that she could do her homework and still have time for music? I think so.

Last is the question of adult leadership. What do we want our children to do with their lives? Many teachers believe in self-motivated learning. This usually means that, from an early age, children should have a great degree of freedom in choosing areas of interest, and those choices often cause conflicts between home behavior and school responsibilities, like homework.

For example, a child in my school had not done some simple homework assigned by her sixth-grade teacher. I received a note from her mother stating that Gina was "at a dance until eleven last night" and couldn't do her homework. Mother came in and promised that Gina's homework would be done from now on. (As if Mother could make such a promise!) The next day, Gina's short math assignment was not done, and the note from Mother said, "Please excuse Gina—by the time her drama lessons ended, we had to go out. Sorry—it won't happen again."

Within a few days, Gina's reading work was not done, and Mother called me to say that she had found the answer to Gina's hesitancy in getting her work done: "Gina told me that she really doesn't like that reading program. That's why she has not been doing her work very well. Could you put her in the other reading group?" I told Mother Diplomat: (a) Gina was in the correct reading group and I would be glad to talk to Mother about changing it but not as a result of her daughter's refusal to do the work; (b) "Gina is responsible for her work. Not you. Please don't write any more notes asking for her to be excused from doing it"; (c)

"Let's sit down together and decide what we would like Gina to learn." I wanted Mother to know that we at school wanted to meet the needs of her child, but that once those needs had been established, we wouldn't tolerate tampering with the program designed to meet them.

The child needs adult leadership at home. This does not mean that the child should be given no choices, nor does it mean that you, as a parent, must ride shotgun over the child, making him or her do homework. But it does mean that you should take an active part in your child's school. Support the teacher on classroom issues. If you disagree, speak up. Teachers are reasonable. But don't show your resistance or disagreement through your child. If you don't agree with the homework, and you make excuses for your child when he or she doesn't do it, you're supporting a cop-out attitude on the part of your child. Once those choices about educational goals are made—by you, the teacher, and your child—there are important lessons that go with them. Give your child those choices, but back them up by seeing them through. The responsibility to see a task through is an important lesson here—not the task itself.

> "But I want peace in my family! I grew up with parents who argued all the time. I don't want that to be the way my child and I live."

Peace at what price? If you let your child have his or her way because you want peace, you may be getting peace at a very high price. It goes back to the very important practice of setting limits. You—and only you—must set reasonable limits for your child. If he or she exceeds those limits, then you must enforce the agreed-upon penalties. Whether or not those penalties include punishment is your decision.

If you give in, even for the sake of peace, what you're doing is saying, in effect, "I set the limits, but they don't count. If you push the issue and threaten this family with war [the opposite of peace], I will go back on my word." When this happens, you, your limits, and your authority are seriously questioned.

On the other hand, some parents can get peace simply by admitting that they made a mistake. It sounds so simple, but if you can admit to your child that you made a mistake, you'll achieve peace, and there'll be no loser, no one to blame, no one using bribes, no one getting bribed. If you've made a mistake, admit it. But if you want peace at any price, you're asking for trouble—more and more trouble as the years go by.

Autocrat-Style Statements

"When I was young, boys acted like boys, and girls conducted themselves in a ladylike manner. I worry about my son and daughter, who are influenced by children whose parents don't seem to care what their children look like or act like. Furthermore, I'm divorced, and I have to work full time. How can I provide my son with a good male image when there's no man at home? And my daughter sees me for just a few hours each day—and when I'm exhausted, at that."

Most parents—single or otherwise—are very concerned about sex role models. With today's new freedom and the frank portrayal of homosexuality on television, I think parents are more bewildered than ever before. The autocrat-style parent does not have a monopoly on clichés like "A boy needs a father," "a mother's love," "Boys will be boys," and "Act like a lady." Let's stop for a moment and try to look at sex role models in a different light. What I'll do is give you some insight into the new way of looking at what being a man or a woman is about.

What do you think of when you hear the word *men*? One of these three categories may come to mind:

A particular, specific man—such as your father, your husband, Clark Gable, or John Wayne.

Things associated with men in general—such as the aroma of Old Spice cologne, the sound of a saw cutting through wood, or weight lifting.

Specific words that describe positive characteristics of men—provider of security, possessor of inner strength, warm, caring, loving, nurturing, and kind.

Now consider the word *woman*. You could think of a woman in any of these categories:

A particular, specific woman—such as your mother, your wife, or Joan Crawford.

Things associated with women in general—the smell of dinner cooking, clothes hanging on the line, or shopping in a supermarket.

Specific words describing qualities of women—provider of security, possessor of inner strength, warm, caring, loving, nurturing, and kind.

Depending upon how you describe men and women, those roles can be very different or almost exactly alike.

> "But I really don't think I *want* my son ever to play with dolls. Something about it seems very wrong."

Your son doesn't have to play with dolls. But neither does your daughter have to play with dolls. Whether or not your son or daughter plays with dolls is not the important issue. How your child plays is the important aspect. Your son needs to learn the human values described above (warmth, caring, loving, nurturing, and so on) in order to function as a human being—a father and husband, if he so chooses. Focus on the values and not objects such as dolls, trucks, or guns.

> "But isn't it important for a girl to act like a lady? I don't want her treated like a tramp or an easy mark when she gets older."

Be careful about expecting "ladylike" behavior! Your daughter has no way of knowing what you mean by ladylike behavior. Children are not mind readers! In fact, we adults probably think of different things when we hear the word *ladylike*. To try to force your son or daughter to live according to preconceived notions is not only harmful but also almost impossible. How can your son know what you mean by manlike or manly behavior? Only by your actions. If your actions cause resentment, you're only hurting your child. A little boy who wants to hug a doll, only to have it pulled away from him because it's not "a manly thing to do," will only resent "manly" things. It scares me to think how many well-meaning autocrat-style parents have shipped a sensitive and gentle son off to military school to "make *a man* out of him."

In addressing the concern expressed in the last example, I'd say if your daughter develops proper, healthy attitudes and respect for herself as a person, you have little to worry about. In short, don't focus on whether or not she wears jeans or likes to go fishing or likes to play baseball. These really don't matter. What matters is whether she likes herself as a person, can say no in a kind but firm manner, and wants to love someone in a meaningful way.

A girl who cannot say no to a boy's sexual advances is one who doesn't know how to say no, to set limits. Were her parents able to say no to her? My guess is that she has really not learned how to say no if she's an easy mark.

If you tell her to stop doing something because it isn't ladylike, all you're doing is telling her that what she's doing isn't wrong, that it's her sex that's wrong.

> "I understand. But I still don't have a husband who can show my son how to grow up like a man."

The message hasn't gotten through. When you think of having a man around as a positive male influence, what do you really want? Do you want a fisherman, all dressed up and ready to bag his limit? Do you want a John Wayne? Do you want a "strong hand," even though you know you should never delegate your personal authority to another? Or do you want a warm, loving, and caring human being?

If you wish your daughter had a woman's touch or a strong womanly influence, what do you really want? Do you want a frilly ballerina? A housewife scrubbing a floor? A bride tearfully walking down an aisle? Or do you want a warm, loving, and caring person?

In both cases, most people would want a warm, loving, and caring person. You can, and must, be the role model for your children, whether they are boys or girls. As I said before, the objects your child plays with are not so important as his or her values. And only you can instill those values in your child.

> "Come on, now. How can a boy who scrubs the floor, washes dishes, does housework—how can a woman respect him? How can he grow up and be a normal man?"

Your son's hormones—unless something is physically wrong with him—will have a far greater effect on his sex drive when he matures than whether or not he scrubs a floor. Many factors can influence sex life, but having Father push a button on a washer-dryer instead of Mother isn't one of them.

Your daughter's ability to grow as a woman will not suffer one bit simply because her mother does things that our culture says men should do. Remember, "ladylike" and "manly" are artificial distinctions.

Any woman who does not respect your son because he washes dishes or does the laundry has a problem. It's not your son's problem; it's hers.

Take a look at your words, your actions. Don't tell your son to act one way, and your daughter another way. It's not easy, because you and I were brought up in a different world, where these differences mattered. Try to be conscious of what you say and do. It's not easy, but it's urgent.

> "My son doesn't do as he's told to do. We make the rules very clear to him, but he refuses to listen. Punishment is the only control we have over his behavior. Can we keep punishing him?"

No, because the punishment will just have to get more and more severe. I am not saying that the autocrat-style parent should become more permissive, because doing that would just be going to the other extreme. What needs to be done, and as soon as possible, is this:

The child—not the parent—needs to start being responsible for his own behavior. If you have a similar problem, here are a few ideas—all parent-proved—that you can use to help your child develop a sense of responsibility.

Take a simple situation: Your son won't turn off the television and come to the table when you say that supper's ready. In your old autocrat style, you might have yelled or physically brought him to the table. Now try this. Announce that supper is ready and that it will be taken off the table if he's not there when he should be. The first time he doesn't come, remove his supper. Don't give in later—you'll ruin what has been accomplished. He won't starve or get sick. This kind of training is called *consequences*. Instead of being punished, your son will soon learn that there are consequences that he—and he alone—will suffer. You will no longer get angry because of something he's done or not done. If you get angry, then it's you who are being punished. When your son misses supper, he will realize that only he can prevent this from happening again—by coming when he's called to the table. Of course, this method won't work with a very young child, so be aware of whether the child is capable of understanding consequences. If he's six, ten, thirteen years old?—definitely!

Try contracts, which emphasize the positive instead of the negative. Contracts work best with older children, who can be expected to carry out the terms set down. But, by all means, don't confuse contracts with bribes. Bribes are sudden, impulsive attempts to get a child to comply through a quick reward that has not been earned. If, for example, your four-year-old is arguing and fighting with another child over a toy, and you give him or her candy to stop fighting, it's a bribe. You've taught the child that fighting is good, because when you fight, you get a reward for stopping. You can't stop fighting unless you start; so you can bet that the fighting will flare up again and again. Second, the bribe is a bad idea because basic human courtesy (in this exam-

ple, not fighting) must be its own reward. To give a child a reward for not fighting or for not kicking the cat is absurd, because
as the child grows older, there will be no tangible reward associated with basic courtesy, consideration for others, and so on.
Satisfaction is the only reward for good behavior. Similarly, the
substitute teacher who promises to give the whole class candy at
three o'clock if they're "good" is making the same mistake.
Whether it's a first-grade class or a high school group, the
teacher shouldn't reward children for behaving as they should.

A contract, in contrast to a bribe, is a well-planned course of
action, whereby a child will learn that there are positive consequences associated with completing a task. When I was a child,
my father gave me a few dollars to wax the family car. Although
our arrangement was never formalized, it was a contract none-
theless. There was a distinct expectation (that the car be waxed
on Saturday morning) and a distinct payment (money).

By using unwritten contracts, you can teach young children
the rewards of a job well done. But you've got to be careful.
Make sure the job is possible for the child to do, make sure the
time limit is reasonable, don't demand perfection, and make sure
you carry out your end of the contract. A five-year-old can contract to have his room all picked up each night for, say, three
days, and he'll get an extra story read to him after those three
days. Your child might say "So what?" to that. If so, use another
payment.

Written contracts are fun for older children. Spell out the
terms (what work is to be done, within what time period, what
the payment will be), and both of you can sign it. Many jobs
around the house can be changed from drudgery to fun this way.
Caution: If the terms are reasonable, and the child fails to carry
them out, the worst thing to do would be to give the child the
payment based on his or her good intentions. Contracts are serious business—fun, but serious. And don't let a contract turn into
bribery, begging, or pleading. Know what you're doing before
you do it. There are many excellent books that go into detail on
the whole contract operation (such as *How to Discipline—with*

Love, by Dr. Fitzhugh Dodson). In any event, don't keep punishing your child and yourself over and over again. Work at changing misbehavior in a meaningful, lasting way.

Many autocrat-style parents I've known are perfectionists, very concerned with order and efficiency. Their expectations are sometimes unreasonable, and, even when a job is well done, they withhold praise until (and only if) perfection is achieved. Consider the case of a child who runs into the house exclaiming excitedly, "Mom, Mom—take a look at this report card!" only to have Mom say, "I just washed the floor—how many times have I told you to wipe your feet?" This child's parent is not only overly concerned with perfection but is killing all the joy present in the situation. Did you ground your child for a week for lying to his teacher—after taking some shady deductions on your IRS tax form? Did you punish your child for lying to you—after encouraging your husband to take a job because "it's off the books"? Does your child hear you tell little white lies to Grandma about how you can't visit her because "the kids are sick"? Take a close look at your own values and expectations. Don't demand perfection of your child, especially when you don't demand it of yourself.

Give your child a chance to be good at something. The child of the autocrat-style parent often feels powerless: only Mom cooks, only Dad paints the house, only Mom may use the new appliance, only Dad may use the new and expensive hammer. Why? Because they want it done *right* (that is, efficiently). What's the message? "Junior, there's nothing you can do right, so that's why you're not allowed to touch anything." Watch those messages you pass on, consciously or unconsciously, to your child.

"Isn't it one of a parent's responsibilities to teach right and wrong? Isn't it important to teach children those values?"

It's certainly important to teach children right from wrong, but what the autocrat-style parent does is define almost every human act as right or wrong. Many things big people (and little people) do are neither right nor wrong. If your five-year-old daughter helps you paint your porch steps and spills paint on the grass, is it really wrong? If your son breaks a new, expensive toy, is it wrong? It may be very frustrating because it may involve added work or added expense, but in neither of these examples can the behavior be considered wrong.

Separate the task at hand from conceptions about what is right or wrong. It might help to think of "right" things as being your thoughtfulness, love, and consideration of your child's feelings. If your child spills paint on the grass, it was an accident. He or she didn't do the wrong thing. It's only human to feel frustrated or annoyed at this. But if you give your child the feeling that his or her behavior is either right or wrong—and that it's usually wrong—he or she will grow up feeling incompetent. You're setting the stage for a child who will feel incompetent as a parent, incompetent as an adult. You won't be providing your child with a chance to be good.

> "My father never listens to what I have to say. I guess he knows the answer all the time, so nothing I say matters to him."

This is not you, you say? Maybe not, but think for a moment of some typical conversations you've had with your children. Have you been thinking of your own concerns, like how you're going to pay back that home-improvement loan, instead of listening to what your child was saying? Are you disinterested when your child talks about wanting a pet hamster or the kind of car he or she wants when an adult?

Do you find that you're in a listening rut? Do you take on certain attitudes every time your child talks to you? Do you have certain pet phrases, such as, "What you want to do is this," "Here's what you should do," "You've got a good idea, but," "Don't reinvent the wheel," "You're burning the candle at both ends," or the all-time favorite "When I was your age"?

Break out of those barriers to real parent-child communication. Force yourself to treat your child with the same courtesy you would show to a customer who walked into your shop. Treat him or her as courteously as you would a letter carrier who stopped to talk after delivering your mail. Surprise your child. Tonight, instead of using one of your usual talk patterns, try this. When your child comes home, or when you come home, actively listen—really listen—to what he or she has to say. Try it. It does not take a minute more of your time, nor does it cost a dime. And it just might get you in the habit of making your time with your child more precious. Isn't that what you always felt a little guilty about—not spending more time with your child? This is real time; honest, human, listening time.

> "When my husband and I make rules, we expect our children to follow them. I don't think children should question everything their parents say. They lose respect for authority and think they are running the show."

There's a big difference between setting limits and enforcing them (necessary in any home) and having rules and regulations that cannot and may not be questioned. Rules by themselves, with no questions allowed, are meaningless to a child.

When we demand that a child obey rules that he or she doesn't understand—"Because I said so"—the child doesn't have any idea as to the purpose for such a rule and, furthermore, doesn't have any idea as to the limits such a rule places on him or her. For example: "Don't ever go into the street" is a rule. "Why?" "Because I said so." "But, Dad, what if . . ." "You heard me. Never." This exchange leaves a lot of unanswered questions: What if Mom's with me? What if you're with me? What if Aunt Sharon crosses the street with me?

Rules like the one above do not guide a child, as rules should. Instead, unquestionable rules place limits imposed by fear. Blanket limits present more of a problem than a guide to behavior. A limit that guides, on the other hand, would be something like "The road is dangerous. You're not allowed in the road alone, only with grown-ups like Mommy, Daddy, or Aunt Sharon."

In her book *Peoplemaking*, Virginia Satir identified key factors in troubled families. Of her four factors, one was "Rules were rigid, inhuman, nonnegotiable, and everlasting." Do these words describe your rule system?

Martyr-Style Statements

"I don't think much of myself as a parent. I feel so inadequate, I just wish I had never had children. They deserve better."

Feeling bad about one's skill as a parent is a common feeling. However, if you're convinced that you're doing a poor job as a parent, the odds are that you feel inadequate as a husband or wife as well. The best advice I can give is for you to talk to a professional counselor or psychologist about it. See what she or he thinks, because these feelings can be just the usual parental worries, or they can be serious. Ignoring a serious problem can be harmful to your child—and to yourself.

But if, like many martyr-style parents, you have these fleeting feelings of inadequacy, don't bother with the whys ("My mother was like that," "My father was insecure," and so on) because the whys won't help you unless you're undergoing psychoanalysis. Think of the whats instead. At what do you feel inferior? What do you dislike about your parent-style? What do you like about it? What do your close friends think of your ability as a parent? What can you do to get a better grip on the parental inadequacy syndrome?

Start with setting aside some time to be with other adults. If you're a single parent, investigate Parents Without Partners, Inc. (see Selected Resources) and seek a close friend or relative to confide in. If you're married, talk over your feelings of inadequacy with your spouse. Having a close, dependable friend to confide in is important—whether you're single or married. Joseph D. Matarazzo, M.D., head of the Medical Psychology Department at the University of Oregon, said: "More psychotherapy is accomplished between good friends at coffee every morning at ten o'clock than all day long in doctors' offices. A good talk with a close friend can solve problems, or at least put them in some perspective, before they become overpowering. One of the problems we face today is the scarcity of good friends."

"I feel as if I have no life of my own. So much of my time is spent doing things for my husband and three children that I feel guilty when I sit and have a cup of coffee. I'm starting to feel that I don't count, that I really don't have a life of my own. I've even forgotten what I used to like to do in my free time!"

Martyr-style parents must break out of this type of situation before they can hope to have any semblance of a personal life. It's so easy to fall into a rut like this—all in the name of giving and generosity. From childhood, we have been taught to share, to be giving and generous—even when we don't want to. Now, as parents, we find more and more of our time is spent as servants instead of as people. This happens to men as well as to women, and it interferes with our ability to be effective parents.

If you've fallen into a rut like this, here's what to do. Take a pencil and paper and write "I count, too!" at the top. What are the many things you're now doing that others must start to do for themselves? List all of them. Do you pick up your teenager's clothing from the floor? Do you lock the car doors for your eight-year-old? List all these things, big and small, that you do. Include things like making beds, washing dishes, cutting the lawn, cooking, shopping for food, and so on, too.

Now organize your day. Decide on the things you want to do, the things you will do, and the things that you feel you must do (remember, you're a person, not a robot).

Some home economics experts say that the average housekeeper should be able to do the day's housework in less than three hours. If you think about it, three hours seems about right. If it seems too short a time to get it all done, you are probably doing too much. Go back to your list and add to it the things that others must begin doing.

After you've listed the work that others must share, organize your day to include no more than three hours, work, and plan other activities—make commitments for your newfound time. You must make that time committed time, or you'll be likely to fall back into the rut of using your time for others. For example, if you've wanted to take a crafts class at the YMCA or YWCA, pay your fee and go. Do you want to join an afternoon bowling league? Do it. It's not enough to think or say "I count, too!" You've got to act upon it. What about the others in your family? You don't have to lay down the law, come on strong, or stop being loving and caring. Just tell family members that you must start thinking of yourself and that some of the work you've been doing alone must be shared. If they won't cooperate, make it clear that the work that must be shared will not get done. You are no longer going to pick up the slack for anyone else.

Working out this "doormat" problem will help make you a happier person and a more integral, respected family member. You will be able to give your family more of yourself if you feel that you're important, too.

> "My children actually blame me when things go wrong for them. When I was first married, my spouse used to make fun of the dumb things I did. But it's not fun anymore. Especially when my children have picked up that same bad habit. Am I to blame?"

This martyr-style parent said it all in the second sentence. By permitting his or her spouse to jokingly poke fun, this parent allowed himself or herself to become the family joke. The martyr-style parent has a double problem here: Not only does he or she get blamed by other family members, but he or she will often be conditioned to accept blame—even when it's not deserved.

A common type of telephone call I get goes something like this: "Mr. DiGiulio, can Greg get hot lunch at school today? I forgot to make his lunch. Tell him I'm sorry—it was my fault." (Greg is thirteen years old.) I've received letters and notes like these: "Please excuse Anna for being late. I forgot to set her clock." "Marianne didn't do her homework because we went out last night. I apologize for any problem this might cause." Not only are these parents taking the blame for their children's behavior at school, they're probably getting blamed at home as well. I can just imagine the scene at home: "Mom, I'm late! Why didn't you set the alarm?" Or, "Where's my lunch? You didn't make my lunch?"

In a recent newspaper interview, Dr. Stella Chess, professor of child psychiatry at New York University Medical Center, was asked, "Can children justifiably blame parents for what they are?" Here is part of her answer.

> For twenty-two years we have followed a group of youngsters from birth to get some answers. . . . We have seen parents whose behavior should have created monsters but produced marvels instead, and we have watched ideal parenting that produced horrors. All children are different and make different parental demands. Some are more difficult than others, and parents cannot be blamed if there is no interaction. . . . It is true, however, that how the parent manages [children's qualities] can either enhance or diminish them. But adults who blame the origins, instead of learning how to best use their endowments, are themselves leading candidates for becoming blamed parents.

Dr. Chess is right on target. The sooner you break your children of the habit of blaming their parents, the better.

Do you apologize when it's not really necessary? Do you routinely say "I'm sorry," even when it's not your fault? Have you written letters to school similar to the ones in the examples? Or had the same thoughts and feelings that these parents expressed? Next time, instead of writing "It's my fault that Fred didn't do his homework," you can write "Fred didn't do his homework." Or, even better, tell Fred to face the music himself. Unless the school has a policy that requires letters (I hope it doesn't!), there's no reason that you have to be Fred's mouth-piece, because you'll wind up taking the blame.

The harder part of changing this whole blame process will be to put a stop to the family's put-downs. The best way to do this is to say clearly and coldly to the offending family member, "I would like you to stop saying those things. I don't think they're funny." This applies to your husband, your wife, or your children. Don't let them slip those put-downs in. You're a human being, an adult, a parent, and you deserve respect. If it's not been given you, demand it.

> "No one listens to me except when I say 'Dinner's ready' or when I get so frustrated I scream. Why am I tuned out?"

Similar to the blamed parent above, the martyr-style parent who gets ignored or tuned out has probably permitted that way of behaving toward him or her to grow slowly over the years. If you find yourself in this position, maybe you've got yourself into a vicious circle. You talk, but no one seems to listen. You repeat yourself but still don't get a response. You say more of the same thing, and the repetition makes people tune you out, and so on. My recommendation is the same as for the tuned-out talker-style parent: Make what you say count. Don't repeat. If someone misses what you've said, it's their loss, not yours.

> "Not only do I feel guilty much of the time, but I also try to make my children feel guilty for the wrong things they do."

Almost all the experts, from Dr. Spock on, have warned against the use of guilt to control children's behavior. There's no question that it's miserable to feel guilty as a parent, but it's even worse to make your children feel guilty. No matter what self-help book or pamphlet you read, it will say the same thing: Guilt is a waste of human energy, a waste of human potential, and totally self-defeating.

The greatest problem parents who feel guilty have is saying no. The next example will illustrate the importance of saying no and provide some tips on how to do it. See the third diplomat statement for more information on saying no.

"Whenever I go shopping, I get a knot in my stomach. My child wants me to buy him everything he sees, and when I can't or don't buy it, he screams or puts up a really embarrassing fuss. I feel guilty because I was deprived a lot as a child, and although I don't want a spoiled brat, I don't want my child to miss out on the things I could never have as a child."

If you mean no, say no. Try it now, regardless of your youngster's age or your own childhood experiences. It will only get tougher as the child gets older. Saying no and meaning it is difficult to do, but it's crucial. Don't worry; your child will not hate you for it. Children are different from adults in that they don't hold grudges any longer than a few minutes. If you have bad feelings about your own childhood, those feelings probably spring from an overall, long-term feeling of being cheated and not, I would guess, from your parents' saying no to you.

Let's look at this matter more closely. For many parents, saying no is not the problem; it's how they say no. How many times have you said "Maybe" or "Maybe later" or "We'll see" when you meant to say no? This hemming and hawing just stalls the inevitable—confronting the child with an honest but firm no. As long as there are at least some yes answers along the way, you've got nothing to fear by saying no. As I said earlier, this is an ideal example of limit setting—so crucial to good discipline.

How to say no is important, but when to say no is vital, too. Obviously, there are times when you must say no. But there are also times when you can give your child a chance to decide for himself or herself, and this should begin as early as the preschool years. Letting children make their own decisions is important because it teaches them to be responsible for the consequences of their decisions; to think through the pros and cons of the choices available; to resist the temptation to misbehave when they're with other children in school; and to apply what they've learned from previous experiences to subsequent decision making. This is the essence of learning how to control their own lives, of learning how to live independently as adults.

At my school, the teachers and I constantly, conscientiously, and carefully allow and encourage children to decide for themselves many issues that in the traditional schools of the past were decided by the teachers. As I said before, children who are constantly told what to do, and who are fed a steady diet of directions, cannot magically grow up to be adults who are in charge of their own lives.

The groundwork for saying no to drugs or alcohol and yes to positive influences is laid before the child enters school. Choosing a course of study in high school, selecting a job from several offered, finding a suitable and compatible marriage partner—all these (and thousands more) require the ability to say yes or no.

Talker-Style Statements

> "Mr. DiGiulio, I know Joey's having trouble with math. I was terrible in math, too. When Joey took that test, he didn't have a good night's sleep. Besides, he doesn't do well in subjects he doesn't like."

In just three sentences, this talker-style parent has summed up his child's ability, desire, and motivation to do mathematics. What he was really doing, however, was making excuses for his son's poor performance in math.

Naturally, this attitude can be very frustrating to a teacher, principal, counselor, or anyone who works with the child. So close is the identification between parent and child that often the parent will not accept any negative statement about his or her child because it's seen as a negative statement about the parent.

This attitude leads to excuses—roadblocks to progress. If Father is convinced that because he was poor in math, his son will also do poorly, the boy is starting out with three strikes against him. He'll probably feel, even before he starts, that he's going to fail. "Why bother at all?" the child may well ask.

"Whenever I want something done around the house, I have to repeat it over and over again. Sometimes I feel that if I've said something once, I must have said it a thousand times."

This problem illustrates the heart of the talker-style parent's problem—saying too much. The following incident, involving a talker-style teacher, is a good example of how the problem develops.

The class was working quietly when the teacher suddenly came upon John, who was working diligently at his desk. Mrs. Green looked to the floor and wailed, "John, the floor's a mess again. Boys and girls, I am sick and tired of telling you to pick up papers from the floor. Why, I can't even walk in this room without seeing a paper here, a paper there. . . ."

You get the message. What this teacher did was disturb the whole class over a piece of paper under poor John's desk. Here's what I told her to do the next time such a situation came up.

"This calls for patience and a bit of self-control, but it pays off in the long run. If John has paper on the floor, as you stand near him, look into his eyes. When his eyes meet yours, raise your eyebrows slightly, point to the floor, and—this I guarantee—John will pick up the paper." In my " 'Guaranteed' Behavior Improvement Plan" for teachers, published by *Teacher*, I call this "the art of the simple technique"—which is very close to the science of making molehills out of mountains. Here's the bonus for using this technique: "No one is disturbed, and John has learned that (*a*) you're gentle, (*b*) you're in charge, (*c*) you smile as a way of saying 'Thank you!' and (*d*) the next time such a situation comes up, he'll feel good about being on your side." This technique can be very helpful for talker-style parents. Try it at home, instead of ranting and raving.

"Mr. DiGiulio, I know you say that Steve behaves himself at school, but you should see him at home. I mean, I don't know what to do. He never seems to listen to anything I say."

I could tell right away what part of the problem was. Steve's mother spoke in a nasal monotone; she had one of the most unattractive voices I'd ever heard. She spoke this way not because of a physical condition but out of habit.

Check out the sound of your voice when you talk to your children. Sit down with a tape recorder and say into it three or four phrases that you use frequently. Now play it back. What do those phrases sound like? Would you want to listen to them all day if you were your child? If necessary, work on changing your voice pattern. Try changing the emphasis (loud at some points, soft at others) and the inflection (don't make all your sentences sound like questions or all like statements). Best of all is this idea: Speak softly and slowly when you're angry. Speak softly when you've got great news. In short, throw your young listeners off the track. Don't make your voice so predictable. Teachers know that one of the best ways to get the attention of sixty ears is to modify the volume and to start speaking v-e-r-y s-l-o-w-l-y. It works!

> "When I correct my child for doing something wrong, she always denies doing anything. She says, 'I wasn't doing anything.' This is so very frustrating to me because I can be looking right at her and she still says that."

In this example, another practical tip from the schools applies. Often a teacher will say, "Johnny, knock it off," or "Johnny, give us a break, okay?" Those phrases aren't effective because they don't pin down or identify the child's misbehavior. I have recommended that teachers (and parents) be very specific when dealing with a child who is likely to deny an accusation. In fact, be very specific in all your commands. Instead of saying, "Johnny, knock it off" (and Johnny says, "I wasn't doing anything"), the teacher could more effectively say, "Johnny, please stop poking Jim. Finish the assignment." What this does is specifically identify Johnny's misbehavior (poking Jim), and it reminds him to stay on task (finish his assignment). Don't get into an argument; neither of you will win. Here's another idea. If you see Johnny—

at home now—poking Suzie, say nothing. Look him straight in the eye and slowly shake your head no. This often works better than any words at all. Remember, make molehills out of mountains.

> "Can I ever be too positive with my children? Aren't praise and kind words the keys to building self-confidence and good behavior? Sometimes, though, I think I praise too much."

Praise is very important. Some children receive no praise at all unless they do a perfect job; their parents withhold praise only for times when children are doing their best. But praise is a powerful tool, and I have seen many talker-style parents fall victim either to praising too much or to praising at the wrong time. The following example illustrates praise at the wrong time. I was walking home from the local general store one morning when I met a neighbor and her young daughter. The daughter was dawdling, and at one point she refused to move at all unless Mother carried her. Mother said, "No, you must walk. Mommy has packages and she can't carry you." After some more delays, the child (three years old) started to hop on one foot, saying, "See, Mommy? See, Mommy?" What did Mother do? She said, "Wonderful! Very good, Lisa." Mother actually put down her packages and clapped. What's wrong here? The child still had not obeyed her mother's command (to walk), deciding instead to show off some skill she'd just learned. In effect, the child not only told her mother that what she says doesn't matter but also got praised in the bargain. Some children are very skillful at manipulating their parents, and Lisa was on her way, for certain.

Another problem with praise is that many talker-style parents tend to praise too freely. Naturally, when babies say their first words, or take their first steps, we want to praise those efforts. And, without a doubt, we should show praise. But, often, parents will forget that their children are now older and require praise less frequently.

A first-grade child did a painting with watercolors, a typical swirl of color, with the overall effect a kind of mottled brown. Little Carmen gave it to her mother as Mother waited at the classroom door to pick her up. Carmen's mother practically exploded when Carmen gave her the work of art. "Gorgeous! What a super job! We have to show this to Daddy! I can't believe how beautiful it is!"

Carmen, looking a bit embarrassed, turned to me and said, "It ain't *that* great!"

12

A Noncreative
Compendium of Self-Help
for Parents

*Romance fails us and so do friendships, but the
relationship of parent and child, less noisy than all others,
remains indelible and indestructable, the strongest
relationship on earth.*

—Theodor Reik

Why do I call this a "noncreative" compendium? Isn't it important to be a creative parent? For one thing, although there is no
one best way to be a parent, there is a multitude of tactics and
strategies that are used with great success by effective
parents.There is little doubt that effective parenthood requires a
variety of techniques, words, actions, and devices—not only to
establish good discipline but also to help children grow into
healthy, self-assured human beings. In short, I say "noncreative"

only to point out that it is not in the ideas themselves but in how you use them that creativity comes in.

It's fine to be a creative parent (and important, too), but how can we even hope to be creative if we're almost constantly dealing with problem children? If we're having difficulty in setting limits for behavior, for example, what good is creativity? If we have to put up with temper tantrums, how can we feel like being creative? Some parents spend so much time dealing with simple disciplinary problems (arguments, bickering, fighting) that they have few honest-to-goodness fun times for themselves or with their spouses and children.

In effect, only parents who have gotten these basics under their belts have the time (and energy!) to spend with their families doing those creative things we hear about or read about in magazine articles. These parents have gone beyond the basics.

Use the following compendium as a basics checklist. As you read, you might wish to circle those statements that you feel are important or the ones that you feel apply to your needs as a parent. Copy those statements and post them in a prominent place. Refer to them, work on them, and make those changes that will help you, too, get past the basics.

1. *Limits.* Set reasonable limits. The key is *reasonable.* When my five-year-old daughter asked me if she could help me paint the outside of the house, my first impulse was to say no. But I knew she just wanted to try the paintbrush, so I asked her to help by painting a strip of clapboard about three feet long. When she was finished with that strip, and only if she finished it, could she do more. I set a specific limit with a clear expectation. This sounds formal, but it's important.

2. *Penance.* Forget your child's past sins or errors. The fact that children forget so much more quickly than adults may be one of the reasons why childhood is looked upon as a happy time for most of us. To dwell on the past is destructive and useless. Help your child to learn from his or her mistakes, but don't turn those mistakes into ghosts that return to haunt him or her. Stop

saying "You *always* do that" when your child goofs. You'll discourage him or her from trying again.

3. *Horror stories.* Don't rely on tales of blood and gore in order to discourage children from running into the street. Be moderate and firm. Telling children that they can get badly hurt or killed is far better than doing a complete description of paralysis and decapitation. A better alternative is to tell them, "You must hold my hand when crossing the street."

4. *Magic.* There's no magic in a child's learning good behavior. Don't expect problems to disappear on their own, and don't place much hope in your child's growing out of a certain unpleasant behavior. How many times have you heard parents say, "It's that age—they all go through it," or, "It's a stage they all go through," in defending poor behavior? A five-year-old child who is very active may be going through a stage, but if he or she is hitting other children, that's just plain bad behavior! A junior high school boy may be clumsy at times and may accidentally break things, but open disrespect to a parent is not "something he's going through."

5. *Actions.* Let your actions speak; rely as little as possible on clichés and empty words. For example, simply telling your child to "be persistent" or that "success comes through hard work" is hardly worth your breath. It is far better to help children gain the knowledge of the meaning of persistence. They can gain it best by your example and your actions. Some parents choose to cart their children to lots of different activities, only to find that these "passions" die quickly, only to be replaced by other fleeting interests. Persistence is the key to, for example, playing the piano. Ask any pianist. Ask him or her if "it all came to you from birth" or in some magical stroke, with no practice required.

6. *Fun, fun, fun.* There is no commandment that says, "Everything thy child doeth shall be fun." I'm not advocating a return to child labor in a sweatshop, but I do want to stress that not want-

ing to do something necessary or important simply because it's not fun is a poor way of looking at life and should not be allowed to influence parents' or children's decisions. Don't let a child evade a responsibility because it's not fun.

7. *Apologize.* When a child has done something that has hurt you or offended another person's feelings, ask for and expect an apology. Teach the child that he or she should say "Sorry"— even if he or she may not truly feel sorry. Eventually, he or she will come to realize that other people's feelings count, and the words will become part of the feelings.

8. *Sugar, spice, and puppy dogs' tails.* Avoid telling your child he or she should behave in a certain way simply because he's a boy or she's a girl. "That's not the way a girl should act" or "Take your punishment like a man" often serves only to frustrate the child. What you're really saying is that the behavior is wrong because the sex of the child is wrong.

9. *Excuses, excuses.* Some parents feel that they must account to their children for all or most of the decisions they make and the actions they take. Don't feel as if you must report to a junior board of trustees. You don't. Explanations, on the other hand, can be important—they are honest reasons. Excuses are disguised little white lies.

10. *When I was young.* Your child can really never know what you were like when you were young and probably doesn't care to hear about how much better behaved you were than he or she is now. If you want to sit around the fire and tell stories about your life as a child, fine. But avoid using them as ways to try to make your child behave better. It won't work.

11. *My family, right or wrong.* A child needs to feel loyal to the family. A brother who sticks up for his brother or sister is making a powerful statement of love. Don't rely on the divide-and-

conquer theory when it comes to your children. Avoid pitting one against the other either by comparing them or by expecting them to rat on each other. Those are poor ways to teach anything, they don't work, and, worst of all, they can drive children apart. Wouldn't you like to be as close to your brother or sister now as you once were? You can help your children to remain close to their siblings by not tampering with their natural love for one another.

12. *Money.* Try for a happy medium on this issue. Do you place too much emphasis on money, or is your child totally unexposed to it? I am still amazed when I meet twelve-year-old children of normal intelligence who cannot make change for one dollar.

13. *Playing favorites.* One of the most powerful ways a child can control his parents is by saying something like "John gets more than I do because he's your favorite" or "You're always letting Susie get away with things because she's your favorite." A comment like that reduces many adults to jelly! Being fair with your children is very important, but allowing yourself to be controlled by their fears of discrimination is simply allowing them to manipulate you. Don't fall for that ruse!

14. *I'm the expert—aren't I?* As your child's parent, you should know what is best for him or her. Does that sound old-fashioned? It isn't. Because if we parents don't know, who does? Is there some special prenatal megavitamin that endows children with life knowledge greater than ours?

15. *A kingdom for my child.* You need not try to give your child "everything I never had as a child" unless what you lacked was a loving parent.

16. *Home, sweet museum.* Is your home a place where a healthy, happy, active child would want to be, or is much of your house off-limits to your child? When I was a teenager, one of my

friends was prohibited from entering the dining room and the living room in his own home. They were roped off with those thick, red velvet ropes you see in a bank. Wiping your feet is one thing, but that was ridiculous.

17. *Can you imagine?* Children's attitudes toward school are largely influenced by their parents. The way parents talk about their children's teachers can greatly influence their children's attitudes toward school. If you criticize the teachers, your child may feel "If they're so bad, why do I have to go there?" In addition, criticizing school or teachers gives children a tailor-made excuse for not trying. "My Mom thinks this school is crummy Why should I bother learning crummy things?" If you want to gossip about or criticize the school, do it with another adult, who can take your criticism with a grain of salt. Children take such matters literally.

18. *Do as I say.* Do you sometimes tell white lies but get angry when your child lies? Do you rant and rave about marijuana when you've got a hangover from last night's party? Be mindful of your ethics; whether you like it or not, they are passed on to your child. The Kennedy Center for the Performing Arts in Washington, D.C., was almost ransacked by people seeking souvenirs. Did "kids" do it?

19. *Loneliness.* Children are often afraid of things that—to us adults—seem minor. Loneliness can be especially distressing to a child. Children need reassurance when they feel all alone. Instead of trying to talk the child out of his or her feeling or trying to convince the child that he or she is not alone, be supportive during these low times. Instead of saying, "You're acting like a baby," try a gentler, more thoughtful approach—"I know you feel lonely," for example.

20. *Authority.* As a parent, you have legitimate authority over your child. Encourage children to respect their grandparents,

teachers, and baby-sitters, but never give your authority to others. Your influence on your child's behavior will be weakened if you permit others to do things (such as spanking) that you and you alone should do.

21. *Television.* Many, many people rail against television. I am one of them. We have read all the gory figures of how much of a child's life is spent in front of the tube. Naturally, instead of encouraging passive television watching, parents should provide stimuli, such as interesting books, games, and puzzles, that will challenge the child.

But, despite what some authorities say, there is one good thing about television. It can help your home situation. If you've reached the end of your rope with your child, instead of blowing up, encourage him or her to watch television. It's better than engaging in open warfare. Whether we like it or not, television is going to be with us for a long, long time. Rather than fighting it, use it wisely—as a temporary baby-sitter, for example, when you're on edge.

22. *The gifted child.* Recognize your child's special needs and do something about them if at all possible. The best way is to go to your child's school to find out what your child's educators recommend. In some states (California, for one), your child is legally entitled to a special education if she or he is "severely gifted." Take advantage of those laws.

23. *The handicapped child.* In every state of the Union, it is the law that your child get a "free, appropriate education." Sometimes schools are hesitant to spend the money that will provide that appropriate education. But it's the law, and, as a parent, you should take advantage of it. First, find out from your child's teacher what he or she thinks is "appropriate" for your child. You'll then have some necessary ammunition to get what your child needs and that to which he or she is legally entitled. Re-

member that this "handicapped law" (Public Law 94–142) pertains to children with reading difficulties; problems with mathematics, speech, hearing, or vision; most physical impairments; behavior problems; and most learning difficulties.

24. *Learn.* One of the very best ways to improve your ability and skill as a parent is to take a course on parenting. In almost every community there are courses for the single parent, courses for Mother, courses for Father, and courses for both parents. You'll not only get some useful information but will also be able to talk turkey with the other students—themselves parents. If you have a particular problem, talk about it with others taking the course. You'd be surprised how common your "unique" problem is.

25. *Consequences.* Help your child to face life's consequences rather than looking for an easy way out. Here's an example. Two boys at my school got into a fight. They understood that the consequences of their actions would be forfeiting their recess time for a few days—a fair, consistently enforced rule. When I called one parent, I explained the rules system about fighting (which her son knew and accepted). She agreed, thanked me, and hung up. Later that evening, I received a call at home from this parent. She told me not to punish her Steven, since "he explained the whole story to me, and it wasn't his fault." This parent had totally forgotten our conversation and the fact that her son had indeed been fighting with another child. In fact, her son was the antagonist. He had other options open to him, but he chose to fight, and now he should face the consequences. There are certain rules we live by (that's why we're "civilized"), and I felt that Steven and his boxing partner needed to learn that those rules are important.

26. *Brag.* Once in a while—don't overdo it—brag about your child. It feels good.

27. *Early bird.* Generally, the earlier in your child's life you begin to instill consistent rules for good behavior, the easier it will

be to provide behavior guidelines in later years. I have never heard of a well-behaved child suddenly turning into a disrespectful monster upon reaching the age of ten. Conversely, the older your child is, the harder it will be to change unpleasant behavior. "Harder" does not mean impossible, though.

28. *Limit your craziness.* I have known parents who get crazy over a certain issue, and that craziness tends to occupy their minds—day and night. Let me give you an example. Mrs. Maxwell's craziness involved a quest for good teachers. Her daughter, Linda, never seemed to have teachers as good as Mrs. Maxwell did when she was a girl. Mrs. Maxwell reminisced often about "dear, blessed Sister Elizabeth, who taught us so well." Mrs. Maxwell often visited the school in an attempt to coerce the principal to get rid of some teachers she thought were poor. Worse, Mrs. Maxwell spoke openly about how poor she thought those teachers were. Did she expect her daughter to be unaffected by her comments? When she asked my advice, I told her to do what she could to make the situation better, but, by all means, to leave her daughter out of Mrs. Maxwell's personal problem with the teachers. Do what you can, but don't let it become an obsession.

My brother, who is an excellent auto mechanic, had a perspective on a similar situation. When I complained to him about my bad luck in trying to get a car dealer to repair the new car I had just bought from him, my brother said, "Bob, I'm in the business myself. I know most of the dealers, and I can't even get them to do a decent job on my car." So what did he do? He fixed his car himself. Instead of complaining (which did no good at all), he accepted the fact that he couldn't rely on the dealer.

Naturally we can't solve our new-car problems this way because we're not all excellent auto mechanics, but the point is this: Do what you can and know when to quit. Don't let an issue become an obsession.

29. *Hug me.* When was the last time, Dad, you combed your son's hair or picked him up? Did you stop holding hands, Mom,

with your son or daughter because they're "too old" now? How about a good-bye kiss in the morning? Corny? Make physical contact with your children as often as possible. Some parents make physical contact more frequently through anger, by spanking or hitting, than they do through loving. Think about it. "Have you hugged your kids today?" says it well.

13

A Chance
to Be Good

A rich child often sits in a poor mother's lap.

—Danish Proverb

If I had to say what I thought was the single most important thing a parent could do, I would say "Give your child a chance to be good." A chance to be good—that says everything. It's a chance to be a good child, a child who is liked and well accepted by others both in childhood and in the adult years ahead. It describes a child who has the ability to love life, to lead a good life—a child who is capable of living life with a satisfied feeling rather than with a defeated, saddened heart and mind.

What's so special about a chance to be good? It's the difference between living a life from one day to the next and almost jumping out of bed each morning in anticipation of the day ahead.

159

Have you ever noticed people who felt that they were not very good at doing things—people who felt that there was nothing special about them—people who felt envious of others who had some special talent, ability, or gift? I've noticed them. And I've noticed that the people who do feel special, those who do feel that they're good at something, or at many things, are the people who seem to live happier lives. And I've also noticed that—in almost every case—these are people whose gifts, talents, or abilities developed or started in their childhood.

Although I graduated from college many years ago, I occasionally hear about my former classmates. As might be expected, the students who have become successful lawyers, respected professors, proficient business people, or competent teachers are the very same people who demonstrated ability and success while in school. Nothing magical happened; they didn't get all the lucky breaks after graduation, nor did they come from wealthy or highly educated families.

There's little doubt that such promise of success starts in a child's earliest experiences at home. It seems as if the seeds of success are already planted in some children even before they start school. In others, those seeds of success start sprouting in high school but usually not later than that. And I'm not talking about the academically gifted child or the child prodigy. Nor do I mean the well-groomed child or the very attractive child. I have seen success-bound children, whether black, brown, or white, in the inner-city schools of New York City. I have seen success-bound children in the schoolhouses of rural Vermont. And what—in every case—seemed to be the key factor?

Mom. Dad. Just one, or both.

Some of those parents were poor, others wealthy. But all of them were aware of the importance of giving their children a chance to be good—a chance to be good at something.

Of course, there were those who meant well: the parents who signed their children up for music on Monday, art on Tuesday, ballet on Wednesday, theater on Thursday, and French on Friday. There were also the parents who told me "My son *will* go to

Annapolis." Some made no effort to hide the fact that they wanted their child pushed or prodded. I guess the purpose was to *make* the child good at something—anything. Arithmetic? "Prod him. He's lazy. He can do it, but he needs prodding." Reading? "Push him. He's an underachiever. Don't be afraid to push him— he's a better reader than he seems to be." These are not parents who give their children a chance to be good.

Giving your child a chance to be good does not mean that you must praise him or her lavishly for every action. It does not mean that you must make your child the center of your life, the center of your universe. You need not enslave yourself. Get rid of words like *devoted, sacrificing,* and *dedicated.* You need be none of these.

Listen when your child talks to you. Praise your child's efforts when they deserve praise. Expect your children to respect the limits you set, but don't set too many unnecessary limits. Limit the dangerous, but never limit the mind. Your children have some wonderful, good, and special things to show you and the world. All they need is a chance.

Bibliography

Sources

Baldwin, A. L.; Kalhorn, J.; and Breese, F. H. "Patterns of Parent Behavior." *Psychological Monographs*, vol. 58 (1945), no. 3. Evanston, Ill.: American Psychological Association.

_____. "The Appraisal of Parent Behavior." *Psychological Monographs*, vol. 63 (1949), no. 4. Evanston, Ill.: American Psychological Association.

Champney, H. "The Measurement of Parent Behavior." *Child Development*, vol. 12 (1941): 131-66.

Crandall, V. J., and Preston, A. "Patterns and Levels of Maternal Behavior." *Child Development*, vol. 26, no. 4 (1955): 267-77.

DiGiulio, R. C. "A Chance to Be Good." *The Single Parent* (October 1978): 9-13.

_____. "The 'Guaranteed' Behavior Improvement Plan." *Teacher*, vol. 95, no. 8 (April 1978): 22-26.

Ford, E. E., and Englund, S. *For the Love of Children: A Reality Therapy Approach to Raising Your Child.* Garden City, N.Y.: Doubleday, 1978.

Lafore, G. G. "Practices of Parents in Dealing with Preschool Children." *Child Development Monographs,* vol. 31 (1945). New York: Teachers College, Columbia University.

Peck, E., and Granzig, W. "How to Tell If You're a Good Parent." *Redbook,* vol. 152, no. 4 (February 1979): 27–152.

Rockmore, M. "Can Children Justifiably Blame Parents for What They Are?" *Hartford Courant* (Hartford, Conn.), July 12, 1978: 41.

Watson, J. B., and Watson, R. R. *Psychological Care of Infant and Child.* New York: W. W. Norton, 1928.

Additional Sources
and
Recommended Readings

Bettelheim, Bruno. *Dialogue with Mothers*. New York: Avon, 1971.

DiGiulio, Robert C. *When You Are a Single Parent*. St. Meinrad, Ind.: Abbey Press, 1979.

Dodson, Fitzhugh. *How to Discipline—with Love*. New York: Rawson Associates, 1977.

Ginott, Haim G. *Between Parent and Child*. New York: Macmillan, 1965.

_____. *Between Parent and Teenager*. New York: Macmillan, 1969.

Gordon, Thomas. *P.E.T., Parent Effectiveness Training: The Tested New Way to Raise Responsible Children*. New York: Peter H. Wyden, 1970.

Satir, Virginia. *Peoplemaking*. Palo Alto, Calif.: Science and Behavior Books, 1972.

Selzer, Joae Graham. *When Children Ask About Sex—A Guide for Parents*. Boston: Beacon Press, 1976.

Smith, Helen Wheeler. *Survival Handbook for Preschool Mothers*. Chicago: Follett, 1978.

Parents Without Partners, Inc. (PWP) publishes an excellent magazine, *The Single Parent*, and the organization is open to the divorced, widowed, separated, or never-married parents who are raising children. There are members in all fifty states and in most Canadian provinces. To find out more about this organization, write:

> Parents Without Partners, Inc.
> 7910 Woodmont Avenue
> Washington, D.C. 20014